Also by Li-Young Lee

Rose

The City in Which I Love You

L
I
•
Y
O
U
N
G

L
E
E

the winged seed

A REMEMBRANCE

Hungry Mind Press
SAINT PAUL, MINNESOTA

ACKNOWLEDGMENTS

I owe an incalculable debt to all of you who, in one way or another, contributed to the realization of this book: Al Giudice, Edward Hirsch, Pei Loi Koay, Philip Levine, Gary Luke, Anthony Piccione, Denise Roy, Rebecca Saletan, Isolde C. Sauer, Eve Servoss, Ileene Smith, Gerald Stern, Jim Thiel, Abigail Thomas, Chuck Verrill, and every member of my family.

And, I ask forgiveness from anyone I may have overlooked.

2:00 A.M., I wake to rain, apartments dark where other travelers sleep.

In my dream my father came back, dressed in the clothes we'd buried him in, carrying a jar of blood in one hand, his suit pockets lined with black seeds.

His gray wool suit seemed hardly worn, except for the shoulders and elbows, which were buffed smooth, I guessed, from rubbing against his narrow coffin. And then I saw his shoes. They were completely wrecked; their leather cracked, nicked, creased, cross-creased; their puckered seams, where the stitching came unraveling, betrayed his naked feet. Sockless, his ankles were frightening, and only the thinnest soles kept him from walking in bare feet.

I began to cry, realizing *He walked the whole way*. I thought of him climbing alone the hundreds of identical stairs up from his grave in Pennsylvania, and then, obeying some instinct, walking west to Chicago, toward his wife, children, and grandchildren. When did he begin his journey, I wondered. In the dream, I felt ashamed, disturbed by the thought that while he looked for me, for us, his family, we were quite unaware of his arrival, which might have taken him years for all I knew, since no one ever told him where to find us. It hurt to think of him walking for years along the blind shoulders of highways, through fields, along rivers, down sidewalks of North American cities and villages; walking day and night; talking to no one; walking; a dead Chinese man separated from the family he brought to this country in 1964; a stranger to most when he was alive; an Asian come to a country at war with Asia; now a stranger in death. I kept looking at his shoes.

The family began to gather for a photo to commemorate his return, during which commotion he seemed distracted; he had an appointment to keep. While everyone stayed busy seating and reseating before the camera, crowding to fit into view, I saw he sat not in his accustomed place, at the center, but, instead, at the end of the front row where he seemed not only comfortable but uninterested. I thought to myself, *I hope his shoes don't show up in the photo. That would shame him, such shoes, and the raw ankle bone.* And then I was certain he'd soon ask me a question and I wouldn't know the answer.

Immediately after the photo was taken, he stood up and walked over to me, who, come to think of it, had been sitting in the dead man's accustomed place. He told me to say good-bye. We had to go. I would be going with him. His words were a blow. I didn't move. Noticing, he asked if I wanted to come with him after all. I answered, *of course.* I lied.

He said, *Very well. I'll wait for you by the locks.* Then
he went out the door.

I looked at the thirteen people I call my family, and
felt suddenly excluded. But then I felt, like miles of water rising in me, a feeling that I could never leave them.

But my father's shoes. How wrecked they were, how
old and battered. I said out loud, *He's so poor. His shoes,
poor father, his shoes.* I felt I should go with him, and began to think over the many names and faces of people
I'd have to say good-bye to, concluding that going with
my father was what I *must* do. But when I walked over to
say good-bye to you, Donna, I could not touch your face.

If it meant leaving, I could not bring myself to touch
you. I began to tremble; trembling, I needed to touch
you. Yet, I could not, no matter what if . . . yet it
meant . . . as it is . . .

Love, what is night? Is a man thinking in the night
the night? Is fruit ripening in the night the night?

I remember fishing with my sister by the light of paper
lanterns, the bamboo jetty at the beach in Ancol. Lying
on our stomachs, we peered over the edge down into the
seawater, and saw, below a surface of many tiny waves,
schools of octopi, their eerie bulb heads glowing.

Night is night as is, without hands. Night is night
even if it's a basin of fire. Night is night though it's ten-
tacle and maelstrom, night even a bloody custard, the
body, dear trough, even if my hand a possible
face . . . night past the color of archipelago. O, how may
I touch you across this chasm of flown things? What

won't the night overthrow, the wind unwrite? Where is the road when the road is carried? What story do we need to hear, so late in childhood? This early in the future, roses exact all our windows, night the wound and way in, night my pink, rude thumb stopper and sink, mustard and ache, my club and good yam, the radish king in his red jacket and green embroidered slippers, writing his letter to the queen of the snails, saying, *I crave your salty foot, suffer me a drink from your horn.* Night, mobile, changes. Though night is night. Even if it's fever and teaspoons, hobbyhorse and train track, the train car empty except for our family and two passengers at the other end, a young woman in a trench coat and the baby in her arms, wrapped in the piss-sodden pages of a Spiegel catalog.

The woman and child had obviously not bathed in days, and the child, who had been bawling on and off for hours, would sometimes convulse, its arms and legs making a frantic swimming in the air, its hands now clawing, now stuck inside its mouth. The woman sometimes opened her coat and unbuttoned her dress to give the child first one breast, then the other, but both were dry. We guessed that both the mother and the baby hadn't eaten in a long time. The woman's eyesockets were bruised by lack of sleep; her teeth and jaw jutted under her skin. The child looked sickly, thin, but its cries were strong. And when it grew exhausted from crying or sucking at its mother's dry paps, it whimpered in her lap, while she stared out the black window, past her own face, to the country passing outside, the country in

l
i

.

y
o
u
n
g

l
e
e

which our family had so recently arrived.

Earlier, at the station in Seattle, we'd seen the woman peel layers of cold newspaper from the infant's naked body, then wrap the freezing child in a drier, more recent edition someone had left folded on the waiting-room bench. The child's sallow, puny body was smeared with newspaper ink. The mother, dirty, gaunt, looked wild.

On the train, she would almost nod to sleep, but the baby squirmed on her knees, nearly falling off, and she would start awake, and pull the child closer. I realize now she herself was a child, not much older than my sister, who was fourteen at the time.

WE HAD BEEN living on butter cookies. We had two tins of them we'd eat among the six of us, my parents and their four children. Butter cookies and the sixty dollars in my mother's purse were to see us through the next few days until my father found work. But my mother decided we could spare the unopened tin. So she untied it from our bundle, and rummaged a sweater from her suitcase and gave the things to my sister to take to the girl, who wrapped the child in the sweater that must have smelled of my mother's perfume. And then the girl began to wave a cookie in front of the baby's face, meaning to feed him. But he, who couldn't have been more than four or five months old, wouldn't eat the cream-colored square held before him.

The girl grew more impatient, the baby bawled

louder. Finally, she, who'd said nothing all along, not a word, not even to hush the child, looked over her shoulder at us and, exasperated, pleaded, "He won't eat." Only my father spoke English back then, and he told my mother what the girl said. After a few seconds, my mother went and sat down beside the girl. She asked if she could hold the child, asked in a language the girl most likely had never heard before, and one mother passed her burden to the other. I saw my mother chew up a biscuit and, all the while humming to the child, and lightly rocking, pass the spit-brightened, masticated paste of her mouth into his.

At first the child didn't take it, but after a few more tries, he ate. The younger mother followed the example. Mouthful by mouthful, the girl fed the child, and eventually they both slept. That woman and child had a further destination than we had that night. When the train stopped in Chicago, we gathered our belongings and walked past without waking them, and continued out through the waiting room of Union Station, and passed through the vaulting arch flanked by statues of two women, one holding her head bowed and bearing an owl on her shoulder, the other raising a naked arm, on which is perched a rooster.

Night is the night and restless. But whose restlessness is this? Mine or night's own? What is night?

My mother and my night are deciding which portion of my fate they'll keep, she in a jar with her celeries and bitters, he in a coat pocket, next to his liver and other vestigial organs. Either she'll divide me with a kitchen knife, or he'll filter me through his teeth. Soon, I may have to rock them both to sleep.

My mother and my night are weighing the separate portions of my fate they own, she as the darker wing to her black hair, he as one more finger to his scary hand. Will she fuss to sew what's mine to me? Will he join me to my shoulder bone? Don't they know I've hidden my fate inside a peach, which isn't round because it's in search of a theme, or a stem, or sugar, or a leaf, but a destiny? Whose night is it forming inside the fruit? Night is the night's peony and monstrous forehead, so our brief bowls, shattered, might spill the sea.

Night is the night carried, death by the rectangular, black-lacquered trunk my father hauled on his back until he got tired, and then my brothers and I took turns shouldering it. It sits now under the living-room window of my mother's apartment, its lid inlaid with jade and mother-of-pearl, depicting a scene from a Chinese opera. I'm dying of the white bedsheet my mother uses to cover it, and the potted white begonia that sits on the sheet, dropping its flowers that lie like lopped ears pressed to a story. Inside the trunk, between many layers of blankets, wrapped in cloth and old newspapers, are the cool jades and brittle porcelains my parents carried over the sea, and a box that used to hold a pair of women's boots. In that box are hundreds of black-and-white photographs of people I've never met, pictures like the one that sits in a gilded frame on the cabinet of my mother's big screen TV. It is a picture of my mother's family, a complicated arrangement of aunts and uncles, first and second cousins, concubines and slaves, and each member sits or stands in strict accordance to his or her relation to my mother's grandfather, the Old President, Yuan Shih-k'ai. It is a feudal hierarchy impossible for me to understand completely, but which my mother grasps at a glance, remembering exactly if it was the Old Man's sixth son, Supreme Virtue, by the fourth wife, Rich Pearl, or the second daughter, Jade something, of the ninth concubine, Have Courage, who killed with a slingshot all the goldfish in the ponds that decorated the twenty acres of formal gardens my great-grandfather owned. And she knows exactly which wan face belongs to the uncle who, forbidden to marry his thirteen-year-old niece, in grief gave up his inheritance, left for Mongolia to live in a hut, let his hair grow to his knees, and wrote page after page of poems and songs about the one called Exquisite Law, who, in the photograph, is carried in the arms of a servant whose face has been blacked out, as all the servants in the photograph have been blacked out, so that the babies they hold (not their own, but the children of the masters) look like they're floating. And my mother remembers who it was that hid among the peonies to avoid having to kiss the corpse of the Old President's fifth wife, who was mourned publicly when she died, as befitted her station. Her fists stuffed with money, her mouth filled with pearls and coins, she was arrayed in her best silks, laid in a coffin of one hundred lacquer coats, and displayed in the living room for one hundred days, during which a procession of mourners, professional and personal, made their way in from the southern door and streamed out through the circular northern portal. Meanwhile, in the chrysanthemum garden, a population of paper figures were erected to mourn in silence this lady who had ruled the fifth household. Her family, as was custom among the very wealthy, had hired artisans to construct out of paper life-size figures of ladies-in-waiting, eunuchs, warriors, scholars, magicians, servants, courtesans, goatherds, and gardeners in every possible posture and attitude of reading, pontificating, viewing flowers, singing, grooming, meditating, sitting, standing, and serving tea. A host of paper mourners and their dogs, cats, peacocks, monkeys, and horses. An acre of figures so detailed and finely made each bore a different expression and distinct hairline. On the one hundredth day of mourning, the day of burial, all of them were to be burned, sent into the next world to attend the old woman whose death had demanded they be cut, creased, folded, and glued into presence. But my mother remembers that on that day, while monks from the local monastery prayed and chanted, sixteen elders banging and blowing shrill instruments in the smoke of thousands of bundled joss sticks reeking bitter sandalwood, a smell only a god could love, clanging and singing amid the smoke, all their words getting blown away on one of the windiest days of the year, while the family members began to dismantle the paper throng in order to carry them to the pyre, a wind came and began to blow the paper statues away. The figures were not made so flimsily that they could not withstand a little wind; in fact, the best artisans were so skilled at their craft that their handiwork could stand for months outside their shops as advertising. But the wind that attended my great-grandmother's burial was so great it lifted an entire paper pavilion, weighing several hundred pounds, along with the members of the court inside it, and straight up carried it away over the walls my great-grandfather had built to enclose the nine mansions of his nine wives and the satellite buildings where the servants were quartered. Family members, frantic, ran all over the grounds chasing paper ladies and paper oxen of assorted colors. But the old lady would have to make her final journey alone, for not even one of those mourners was left intact. The wind set them all free, and tearing.

WHEN MY MOTHER, Jiaying, is a girl in China, she loves the summers in the mountains. The rest of the year, she lives in the city below, in the haunted mansion ruled by her father's mother, a woman as cruel as she is small and desiccated, and as selfish as her feet are twisted to fit into tiny hoof-shaped shoes of brocade. It is because of this woman, my mother insists, that drafty ghosts inhabit the countless rooms and myriad corridors of the old house, whose ceilings and rafters are so high that light never reaches them, giving Jiaying the feeling of living perpetually under a great, dark, impenetrable hood. It was from the rafters in the sewing hall, the darkest room in the entire complex, that a maid, fourteen and newly hired, hung herself after only three months of waiting on the old woman.

The sewing hall is a building whose front face is wood and whose other three walls are windowless brick. Two double-door front entrances lead into a cavernous room of stone floors and two rows of three pillars each, painted thickly red, and spaced ten feet apart. Lined with tables at which thirty women sit behind mounds of various fabrics of any color, the room whines and rings with the rapid pounding of several hand-operated sewing machines. Forbidden to wear against their bodies any piece of cloth cut or sewn by men, all the female members of the nine households have their clothes made by women in the sewing hall. Thirty seamstresses, every day all year round making and mending the clothes of births and deaths for every female Yuan, cutting and sewing from patterns handed down generation to generation without mutation for nearly a century, so that almost everyone in Tientsin knows that the less fashionable you are, the older the money you come from. Thirty indentured workers, bought or born into bondage of cloth, sew in the great hall, drinking little cups of tea that amount to green seas, gossiping and telling stories. All day long, necks bent and fingers crooked to meticulous mending or making, by machine and by hand, embroidering, and weaving, and stitching, threading endless miles of spooled thread of all different colors and thicknesses. All different ages, the workers sit according to years of servitude and age, the oldest, having been there the longest, and whose eyes see the least

the winged seed

after years of strain, sit at the front of the room where there is the most light from the windows and doorways, while behind them in progressive densities of shadow sit the younger and younger ones less and less blind. Deepest, where the sunlight never reaches, sit the youngest ones, twelve and thirteen, the newly arrived, the tenderest with their sharp, clear eyes, sewing in shadow. Soon enough, though, they'll get to move forward more and more as the very oldest grow so blind they have to quit, just as they themselves, the younger ones, will see less and less, even as they move nearer and nearer the sunlight. By the windows sit a few women old and almost completely blind and whose hands are so twisted as to be not recognizable as hands anymore. Useless and used up by years of service, they tend to the countless cats that live in the sewing hall. Cats of all different sizes and shapes and colors, living on a gruel of rice and fish, or mice, or sometimes their own litters, they far outnumber their keepers, none of whom knows how they came to live there in the first place. Nameless and nondescript, they endlessly prowl along the walls and the legs of the tables, so that the workers sense a constant motion at their feet, a continual brushing past of fur.

Jiaying hates the sewing hall because of the cats. She hates the smell and the hundreds of little eyes behind the tables and in the shadows. She hates the countless tails curling and brushing past her when she is there on an errand. There are so many of them they can hardly be called pets. The ones who have the job of tending the brood sit by the windows sipping tea, chewing their

l
i

•

y
o
u
n
g

l
e
e

gums, and squinting. The oldest of them, who swears she
remembers having sewed the President's scholar's robe
for graduation, sits absently grinning to her toothless
self. Whether she is recalling better days, or smiling in
the knowledge of the fate of all those young pretty girls
in the back, no one can tell.

It was here one morning someone looked up into the
ceiling and there, where the swallows build their high
unseen nests in the dark of the rafters and brackets, was
one white sock dangling in midair. It was the white-
stockinged foot of someone hanging from the rafters.
Screaming and turning over chairs, the women cleared
the sewing hall like frantic birds sprung from a box.
Members of the nine households assembled in the yard
and someone took the body down. The fifth wife's new
maid had hung herself. Judging by all signs, she'd done it
early in the morning. It must have been just light when
she climbed up on a chair set on a table and scaled the
rafters and scaffolding. Everyone speculated on what in-
sanity made her go to so much trouble to hang herself
from the highest ceiling in the whole complex. For days
afterward everyone kept looking into the ceilings of
whatever room or corridor they were in. And then people began to see the girl walking around. Even Jiaying's
grandmother, who used to make the girl stay awake entire nights rubbing her feet, and beat her pitilessly if she
fell asleep, claimed to have seen her once, but just once.
She said she woke from a restful afternoon nap and had
the feeling someone was in the room. Furious to have an
uninvited guest, she opened her eyes to find the Little

Ugly, as she was fond of calling her because of her pocked face, sitting next to her. *What did you do, Nai Nai?* the granddaughters gasped who were listening to the story. *What do you think I did?* she gloated. *I told her if she didn't behave I'd make her mother who sold her to me my maid as well.* The girl never visited the old lady again, although others continued to see her.

But, *Let's not talk about old things,* is my mother's response most of the time I ask her about her childhood. *Don't make me go back there. Like those evil-smelling, greenish black potions the servants cooked and served hot to me in winter for coughs and headaches as a child, the past is all one bitter draft to me,* she says as my sister combs my mother's hair in the morning, by the window looking onto her garden. When I press her, she says, *I can't tell if your head is an empty house, or a pot of boiling glue,* and then inserts the alabaster comb into her loosely piled-up hair, a black nest, and waves a silver stray back with her hand summarily, as though to dispel so much cobweb or smoke. *Now let's go buy some fish.*

At the Beautiful Asia Market in Chicago, the refugee grocer is a bent, brown-colored man with a big black mole on his right jaw, and the fish tank is empty, except for some filthy water. The only fish I see are two carp afloat in a bucket propping a mop in it. So we'll buy the gnarled man's perfectly trimmed napa cabbages, but have to get our fish elsewhere. *Elsewhere,* my mother says, *your head is always elsewhere, in the past or in the future. Why can't you be here?* I wonder about an answer while I push a tinny cart with a crazy wheel down the

l
i

•

y
o
u
n
g

l
e
e

fragrant lanes of tea, aisles of lemon grass and sandalwood, musty narrows of spices and medicinal herbs, rows
of shelves, and shelves of jars of chopped pickled mud-
fish and shrimp ferment, soybean paste and preserved
monkfish, eel eyes staring out from brine, sealed stacks
of biscuits and cocoa from Belgium and England, and
cartons of instant noodles stacked to the ceiling. I
browse with my mother, each of us keeping the same
things we need for dinner as different lists, Chinese and
English, in our heads, and my mother, because her eyes
are bad, inspecting the goods with a spyglass.

In my mother's dreams, she wanders that old ground,
the family compound, and it's evening, and becoming
more evening. She's on an errand to the sewing hall, and
the cloth in her hands is poorly folded. And I know by
her description that it's the same path I walk in my own
dream. In my mother's dream, she walks in the general
direction of the sewing hall, but avoids it. In mine, I'm
sitting on the steps and the doors are locked. In my
dream, I sometimes stand among trees the way I stood
three summers ago on Fragrant Mountain, and look
across the valley to another mountain face, where my
wife leads our children up a winding path. Below, my
grandfather's bones scattered by the People's Army.

In my mother's dream, she is again a girl of sixteen in
China, where she spends summer with her family on
Fragrant Mountain, making the final two-day leg of the
serpentine ascent through dense forests on muleback, in
a train of twenty-five mules bearing her father, her
mother, her father's concubine, three aunties, one

brother (the other having been banished by the grandmother), two of her sisters, fourteen and thirteen years old (the other two attending boarding school in France), her favorite cousin, the same age as her and recently orphaned, two of her brother's friends whom he met in New York while attending school there in the fall at Columbia University, three bodyguards armed with rifles and pistols, four household servants, one cook, three dogs, and various equipment and supplies. On the trip up the narrow path, while one of her sisters reads aloud from Zola or Balzac, Jiaying nibbles on fresh lychees, which they carry up the mountain. The mule bearing the burden of Jiaying's favorite fruit can't tell as that burden imperceptibly and gradually lightens, as Jiaying fills her mouth with its sweetness.

When she is a little girl in China, Jiaying's favorite food is lychee. For one brief season a year, the markets are full of that globose, hard-skinned fruit tied in pink string at the bundled stems, and her father sends the servants to buy them for her each morning. Unlike all the other fruits that smell and taste of sunlight compacted, then mellowed to sugar, lychee yields to her tongue a darker perfume, a heavy redolence damp with the mild edge of fermentation. How wonderfully fitting it seems to her that such milky, soft meat should be surrounded by a rough, brown reptilian leather of a slightly red cast when ripe, and made almost impenetrable by being covered in tiny rivets and studs. Summertime, she grows thin on nothing but lychee flesh. She waits each morning for the servants to bring bundles of it home, and rather than have the fruit peeled and served to her in a porcelain bowl that fits precisely the bowl of her hand, she prefers to peel for herself the tough skin, rough to her fingers. Using her fingernails to puncture the exterior, she splits it open and takes with her teeth the white meat slippery with nectar, the whole plump bulb of it in her mouth, and eats it to the smooth pit, which she spits out, leaving on the verandah each morning a scattering of black stones and empty husks, sticky with sugar and swarming with bees. A servant sweeps the verandah, scolding her.

Ordinarily forbidden to go out beyond the confines of their home, a complex of nine mansions and attendant satellite buildings housing the families of the nine wives of Jiaying's grandfather, Jiaying and her sisters' only contact with the rest of the world has been for years through the private school they attend, where they make friends with girls who, while their families can afford the cost of private school, do not belong to titled households of rank, and who, as a result, are not bound to traditional ways and attitudes the same way Jiaying and her sisters are so strictly bound at home. When each of the Yuan sisters distinguishes herself in her studies, and is encouraged by her parents and her grandmother to continue her education after middle school, naturally, each of them takes advantage of the opportunity by enrolling in fashionable French and British boarding schools. All five of them except Jiaying, the oldest, who decided to stay home, where everything that surrounded her was so old, she was certain it must be permanent. The poems she read were thousands of years old, the calligraphy she practiced was practiced by smart refined girls like her thousands of years ago, the house she lived in and the grounds surrounding it looked to be as old as anything else in the whole country, and as half buried. During the summer sand storms, when all the tiles, the latticed windows, the carved railings and figured eaves were packed with sand, and little dunes formed against the buildings, she knew it was sand broken off eternal mountains and then driven the whole way from the Gobi, that old fabled desert, and was on its way to that most ancient of bodies, the sea. And her grandmother, only forty-five but already walking with the aid of a cane and three or four servants, seemed to be some eternal fixture in the universe with her medicinal odors and old ways. How could she conceive of a future when everything around her felt like the end of things, the world's very culmination.

Of all the things packed onto the sweating mules, Jiaying writes in her diary dated June 6, 1939, *an individual lychee is probably the lightest. Or else the calligraphy brushes. Only the little bamboo-handled goldfish nets are as light as the brushes. Next would certainly be the butterfly nets. Then Auntie's opium in its beautiful paper wrappings. Then the pipes. The weight of the rest of the things is distributed as evenly as possible: zithers and lutes, flutes, Ba's typewriter, and tea, mirrors, telescopes, fishing poles, and jars of embalming fluids, empty bird cages, dictionaries and books in Chinese, English, and French, subjects ranging from poetry and astronomy to* The Art of War, *and magnifying glasses,*

boxing gloves, chess and mahjong sets, bows and arrows,
slabs of salt- and sugar-cured meats, squat clay pots sealed in
wax holding assorted preserved fruits and vegetables, and
pages of rice paper bound in boards, ink blocks, and a mon-
key to grind the ink.

They ride slowly through increasingly clearer air,
making frequent stops to picnic, shoot small game, and
take photographs. The cool, immense night they spend
at a rest station manned by servants they sent ahead
days ago to prepare for their arrival. By candlelight, Jiaying writes in her diary, which she reads to her cousin:
Miles up from the city. Many more miles to go. Here a place
to rest. Ahead, another. And farther, another.

Their last stop before reaching the summit is the an-
cestral graveyard. An acre of meadow bounded on three
sides by woods and on the fourth by the gravekeeper's
small farm, on it stand the twelve-foot-high marble
headstones of various shapes. The cemetery gate is a
huge nail-studded crossbeam set by wedges into twin
two-story posts hewn from whole trees, the entire thing
tooled and painted with patterns, symbols, and signs resembling eyes or flowers or clouds, and flanked by a set
of stone mythical beasts. Half dog, half lion, half scowl-
ing, half grinning, standing on their platforms taller
than the gravekeeper's house, both guardians look as
though they were peering over his roof.

Once at the site, Jiaying and her family burn incense
and paper money, and pray to a long line of illustrious
men and women whose severe portraits hang huge and

forbidding in the tall, gloomy corridors of their home in Tientsin, a city far below them now as they stand in a high meadow in the mountains.

In the whirring and clicking of grasshoppers, they walk at the feet of the white marble stele. On each is carved a poem commemorating the one who lies underground shrouded in countless layers of silk and enclosed in a box filled with money and precious jewels. As well as flowers, birds, and animals, human figures are etched in various depictions of filial piety. Even as Jiaying stands bowed at the foot of a stone slab two and a half times her height and wide as a double door, above her eternally is the figure of a young girl not unlike herself, clothed in a style hundreds of years old, paying her dutiful respects to the unanswering dead.

While Jiaying and her family linger over the names and poems, no one thinks that Jiaying's father and grandmother will be put in this ground soon. Even less would any of them believe that on an afternoon years from now, a group of student revolutionaries will casually pass through the gates of this place, and dig up the graves and rob them, dragging up the corpses of her father and grandmother to strip and tie them naked to a tree. Jiaying, who will have left the country by then, will have to hear about it almost half a century after the fact, from the gravekeeper himself, who after so many years still recognizes her, and falls to his knees to bow to her, calling her by her title, when she comes back here a woman. She'll have arrived by car then, accompanied by her own children, her husband dead, to be greeted by the man who has lived on this farm ever since the one day he climbed up the mountain to work for her family and never came down again. He'll walk with her over the ground, which has been turned into a pig farm. A few feet behind one of the sties, he'll take her through shoulder-high cannabis plants to see the few smashed and overturned monuments that haven't yet been removed. She'll stand in the glare of afternoon and squint to make out the pieces of names and poems in stone. She'll walk ahead a few feet and suddenly find herself standing dumbfounded at the gaping pits of concrete vaults of defiled graves. Then the old man will show her where he buried her father and grandmother after he untied them from the trees. He'll point to a strip of ground under three feeding troughs, apologizing that he can't remember who is under which trough. *But they've all been punished by heaven,* he assures her. One by one, he says, the looters died from wearing the silks they stripped off the corpses.

In my mother's dreams, she is always shocked to find the graves gaping. In mine, I'm sitting again in a green pavilion in the park in Ho Ping District, drinking tea of leaves my nieces picked in the mountains north of Tientsin, nibbling dates my uncle has brought back from Turkey, where he sailed with a cargo of radios. I'm playing go at a card table with my cousins Shwen-dze, Man-dze, and old Lao himself, go-masters every one of them. In my mother's dream, she sews a sail for a boat. In mine, I weave all day in view of night. Come night, I'm all alone, the material coming undone in handfuls of human hair.

Is night my ancestors' gloomy customs, then? Will I ever be free of their tortoiseshell combs and smoking punk, hand-tooled jambs that stalled and amazed me at temple thresholds in a provincial capital? Will I be free of my great-grandfather's three thousand descendants? Soon, there will be so little of me I may actually arrive. Soon, I'll be born. Soon, I'll know how to live. Soon, my teeth may stop hurting me. Soon, I'll be able to sleep. At the moment, something I never read in a book keeps me awake, something the night isn't saying, the wind is accomplice to, and the rain in the eaves keeps to itself, an unassailable nacre my woman encloses, a volatile seed dormant in my man, something I didn't see on the television, something not painted on billboards along the highways, not printed in the magazines at the supermarket checkouts, something I didn't hear on the radio, something my father forgot to tell me, something my mother couldn't foresee owns an unbroken waist and several ankles, a stem proclaiming an indivisible flower, a lamp sowing a path ahead of every possible arrival.

How many nights have I been nudged awake by some thought, like a boat evenly rocking suddenly bumped from below, and hearing the hems of gowns shift outside the window, turned to my wife beside me and said, *It's raining,* and she answered by setting her sole's arch against my instep. How many nights have I lain here like some drowned cabin of a ship through whose portals fish big and small swim in and out in the dominion of the octopus and clam, and allowed myself to remain an unguarded room, open to thoughts coming and going, passing head to toe, no single thought as shapely as the course of a various thinking, no one idea as grave as this dark traffic, in whose current I drift, wondering, Did I close the windows downstairs? What time is it? Is the basement flooding? Did I put the garden shears away? Did I leave them in the rain to rust? Did I finish writing that letter to my father, or did I let the pencil fall from my hand? My love, why can't you sleep? Why does each night lead into a sister night? Is there nothing one can say about tonight or any other night the night won't unravel, every effort undermined by night itself? What were those seeds doing in my father's pocket? What is a seed?

I remember, as long as I knew him, my father carried at all times in his right suit-pocket a scarce handful of seeds. *Remembrance,* was his sole answer when I asked him why. He was pithy. He slept with his head on a stone wrapped in a piece of white linen I washed once a week. Up until I was nine years old, I napped with him, making myself as small as possible so as not to wake him. I remember how, when he turned over in bed, I made room, wedging myself against the wall, my left arm under my head for a pillow, my legs numb. I lay very quietly while he snored. I lay wide awake against his flesh while he slept with his head on the stone wrapped in the cloth which smelled of his hair, a rich oil. When he died, the stone kept a faintest impression that fit the shape of his head. My mother carried it out, and left it under one of the thirty-six pines that enclosed two sides of the property on which our house stood, the third side the fence where the morning glory climbed. Some days the depression in my father's pillow must fill with rain, just enough to give a cardinal a drink. Or maybe somebody has found it by now, has used it as part of a wall, where it fits to another stone shaped like a man's skull. We burned most everything else before selling the house and moving. Out of the heap of his papers, notebooks, manuscripts, photographs, and letters, my sister Fei, almost obligingly, chose one scrapbook of newspaper clippings to keep, which none of us ever looked at after we left Pennsylvania. Everything else we fed to a roaring fire we'd made in the backyard between two apple trees. While we all stood about the fire, which we kept alive two days and two nights without sleeping, one hot mote shot out and creased my youngest brother's thigh, burning through the cloth of his pants and several layers of skin. His leg owns the scar to this day.

l
i
•

y
o
u
n
g

l
e
e

I NEVER ASKED my father in remembrance of what he kept those seeds. I knew better than to press him when I was a boy. Now I'm a man, and he is dead, and I feel a strange shame that I don't know what happened to those seeds. Did we bury them with him? Is morning glory breaking his pewter casket's tight lip this second? Is morning glory blooming on a cemetery hill in Pennsylvania? Didn't I one day kneel in the mud and snow, halfway up a hillside, halfway to my father's grave, and hold my wrist to an icy cataract, and see the shriveled vine and the gold seed pods?

Or was that last night on the stairs? A bird, perched on the spindled rail, asked the time. Or else told it, according to a stone of boundary, the dead moon, and a stone of next news, the seed. Deaf water fell unseen. Steep, it numbed my mouth, when on the stairs of an unfinished house I drank it, and you asked, my love, why can't you sleep? But I can't say. What restlessness is this? Is this the restlessness of the needle or the cloth? The wing or the journey supporting it? The oarlocks or the rower's arms? Does my hand move over your body to precede me home, and do I therefore, by its continual departure, arrive?

Nights like these I'm host to passenger seeds, burrs, and black hats. I'm that abandoned shed my sister and I came upon when we were children on the island of Java. One wall bore a poster of Sukarno, and it stood derelict, home to birds and lizards. With a spoon, we dug a hole in the dirt floor there and buried a jar of rupiahs we promised to return for, thinking for some reason our treasure would triple in the ground. Climbing in by one window, we left by climbing through another. Or I am like the broken-down shack in East Vandergrift, Pennsylvania, where Charlie November lived, the sloping front yard strewn with broken car parts, the table inside scattered with shotgun shells, the twelve-inch black-and-white TV on all day, and Charlie gone. The shed was built on the side of a hill at the edge of that rivertown's limits. I remember summer evenings when I stood for a moment in his doorway and looked at the view he owned, the whole wide river valley. In the proper season,

I could witness hundreds of dandelion seeds float slowly over the valley, each carrying a spark of the late sun, each turned to gold by what it bore from one side of the river to the other.

I hold in my left hand a morning glory seed, a hard, wedge-shaped, odorless stone the size of a tear. My love, what is a seed? Is it its flower? Is it the leaves it utters? Is it a house? Where is the honey hidden, in which room? Where is the owner? How much room is a flower to a bee? Who could tenant a house so narrow as a seed? Only the least among us could live there. Its weight is imperceptible. Lighter than the flower, it is where the flower closes at evening. Yet, in it may be growing the flower that will overthrow all governments of crows or senators. This seed comes to divide me from all I thought I knew. This seed revises all existing boundaries to proclaim the dimensions of an ungrasped hour. This seed carries news of a new continent and our first citizenship, and I hold it.

Tonight, I am its ground, though my hand can hardly endure the next world lying inside it. And I must overcome my urge to whisper something to it, tell it something only a seed could hear, or something a seed has never heard, a human thing.

But if a seed is a house, is it a finished house, or the house unfinished? Is it my father's house? No. My grandfather's house? No. Has the clock in the hallway stopped? Will I have to get out of bed soon and wind it? Or have I, between two crests of the swinging pendulum, fallen asleep? What is night? Is it a ladder? Do we double the night who sit inside it? Or does night pass through us on its way to fruit and other immensities? Does night own a hammer? Or does night build without equal? Are there more than two nights, yours and mine? Is that my father in his undershirt, bent at a table, studying a sentence, darkening the lamp? Is that my father cutting out pieces of colored paper to make lancet-shaped windows, the lamp and the scissors-bird winking and seeming to fly?

His one hand holds the scissors and slowly squeezes it closed, while feeding into its blades with his other hand the folded tissue papers colored red, yellow, green, and blue. Turning the little stack of them along the faintly penciled lines, he lets fall a little shower of tiny bright leaves. These he glues to the pieces of one-eighth-inch-thick cardboard he's painted gold, and into which he has already cut the window openings. Three identical walls and together they made the sides and the rear of the temple.

What it took a great king seven months to accomplish with stone and three hundred thousand slaves, it took my father nearly four years to complete out of cardboard and paper, a feat of love, or someone serving a sentence. *And there it is unto this day.* The speaker of the sentence is referring to Solomon's Temple. The sentence follows a long and detailed description of that fabulous house of the covenant. And *where* is it this day? One must not ask. Where is that magnificent temple? For it lives only in the sentences of its description, and only inside the imagination of the reader of those sentences.

He'd begun the project as a gift for my sister when she

t
h
e

w
i
n
g
e
d

s
e
e
d

turned eleven on the ship to Macau. That winter, Ba was being transferred from the prison in Jakarta to another in Macau. We would not get there, and Ba would not finish the gift in time for his daughter's birthday. Instead, due to a series of oversights and accidents on the part of the Indonesian War Administration, as well as a friend's timely arrival in a secret boat, we would end up in Hong Kong for Christmas, where construction on my father's temple continued; and then Japan, where building went on; then Singapore, and on, and on, each place new, while one thing remained the same: on a ship or in a tiny apartment room, a table was cleared where my father bent alone over his Bibles and dictionaries, translating his books of Genesis and Exodus; or else his wife and children sat by him while he resumed work on his temple.

There was no rest. Mumbling in Hebrew, Greek, English, and Chinese, Ba was moving us from one place to another. And he was building as we moved. What began as a toy for his daughter became the sole activity around which the family gathered, no matter where we lighted for a week or a month. And the real genius of the thing was not only its true-to-life, full-scale construction, nor its swinging doors complete with bolted locks, nor even the tenderness in the details of the faces of the seraphim, but its portability. For each piece could be gently dismantled, unfolded, spread flat, and put into a box to be carried across borders, barriers, into provinces, jungles, over seas and lands as language to language, landscape to landscape, we carried Ba's Temple of Solomon.

And Ba was dying. Something terrible must have happened to him during his time in prison, for he left that place damaged. Something about him persuaded us he was in the last of his wholeness. And the close air we shared in holds of ships and trains and little tenement rooms dogged us, his woman and children. Our clothes smelled musty, our shoes grew tight even as they disintegrated, the pages of his dictionaries grew yellow and water stained, our bodies smelled like . . . dying. We slept the sleep of the dying. We ate the food of the dying. We saw sores begin to erupt all over Ba's body. We feared, at one point, it might be a form of leprosy. We heard him complain about severe aching in his joints. Yes, Ba was dying. And we were dying to arrive, to put behind us the dying on the islands, the rounding up and dying en masse. So we made our escape. Out of forgeries we made our flight. Out of accidents and silences, out of the steps of the fleeing who went before us. And though our course seemed aimless, decided by nothing but fear, Ba assured us it was momentous, even predetermined. Our seemingly incoherent and stray rovings across the horizontal plane of seemings and doings were, in fact, he convinced us, a continuous unfolding of vertical and ultimate meaning. And since the nature of moving is collecting, naturally, we collected: curly sea foam, scaly archipelagoes and leafy rain, lunatic moths, jeweled eyes of snakes, curled tails of monkeys, and the fangs of the monkey king, two snakes coiled on the back of a turtle, a cream-colored gecko uttering a concrete cipher, dawns the color of evening gongs, temple bronzes that owned the look of things having been too near the sun, black zones of one or two seas, *thank-you*'s and *please*'s in different tongues. On Ba's scuffed, cracked leather accordion case, we collected colorful stickers of steamships and airplanes, and emblems of airlines and train lines and shipping lines, our whole wandering pieced together by such lines, the only continuity our bodies in time, and Ba's relentless work on his temple. We saved and collected anything at all that might be of use, from thin, colored tissue paper to the foil from cigarette packs or the beautifully colored envelopes of Christmas cards. And Ba built it. While Ba and Mu collected lines on their faces, he built it. While Fei, Go, Be, and I accumulated body weight and size, he built it. According to the instructions God gave to Solomon, Ba made it, his own splendid temple.

The front wall bore a wide, double-door entrance on either side of which was a tight grouping of four windows. And around every window of all four walls, my father cut with a razor a beveled edge to make a frame, exposing the gray cardboard beneath the gold paint. Then, around each frame, in fine lines of black ink, he decorated the windows with minute curlicues, leaves, vines, scrolls, waves, human and animal figures, no two sets of windows bearing the same motif, no two leaves of a single window alike.

The lintel and jambs of the doorway, as well, were embellished with profuse and singular details, indicating the obsessive and aching hand of a maker whose playfulness was surpassed only by his determination. The surface of the cardboard double doors was scored and cut to

l
i
.
y
o
u
n
g

l
e
e

look like thick planks of wood, while the studs and horizontal bands of metal lashing the planks together were
made from colored construction paper. These were the
walls of the outer sanctuary, which was further surrounded by colonnades. The columns were made by
scoring with a razor blade a series of close vertical lines
on a piece of cardboard, which was then folded along
the lines to make a fluted shaft. Because the entire project was designed to be dismantled easily, the shaft was
attached to a simple base and capital by a system of tabs
and slots. Fourteen such columns supported a pitched
roof whose gables were adorned with detailed renderings
of scenes from the Old Testament up to the time of
Solomon; mainly depictions of trials and slaughter. The
roof itself could be lifted off to reveal the inner colon-
nade of the inner court, at the center of which stood the
pillars Jachin and Boaz, guarding the cella, the final and
innermost room in which knelt the two six-winged
seraphim brooding over the Ark of the Covenant. The
entire project sat on a cardboard stage ascended to from
any direction by six such stages of succeeding size.

But where is it now? Gone. Like everything else. And
even while we were moving, I was moving to eventual
awareness that all was not right, that all we ended up
amassing was ephemera: songs in languages we didn't
know, memories of fragrances of indeterminate flowers,
loose chants and charms, silhouettes of huts and
minarets; while Ba was reenvisioning Genesis and Exodus. We carried our clothes in bundles, our books and
shoes were rotten. We were sleeping standing, eating

squatting, putting the bowl to our lips, while Ba meticulously scissored, folded, tucked, and layered into existence his house of worship, while his little, gold, indomitable watch tolled the relentless hours. And naturally, we were casting off as we looked ahead. We were jettisoning luggage, names, and bodies. There was Tai, my brother. Then there wasn't. There was Chung, another brother, then there wasn't. Brothers swallowed up in some murk we called, conveniently, The Past, as though it were a place we could return to, as though we weren't leaving them behind with the passports we left behind, the jewelry and the books come finally undone. As though making the faces of the seraphim in the exact likenesses of Tai and Chung were a suitable memorial. And we were waxing tired, waxing bewildered, for we were departing in order to leave, leaving in order to leave some more, some more tired, some more old.

And by the time we got to America, my feet were tired. My father put down our suitcase, untied my shoes, and rubbed my feet, one at a time and with such deep turns of his wrist I heard the water in him through my soles. Since then I have listened for him in my steps. And have not found him. Since then I hear with my naked feet, those lilies, fine-boned swans crossed at the necks, those ears. My father's feet were ulcerous, as was his body, diseased. And water denied him days at a time, administered in a prison cell in Indonesia, ruined his kidneys, and changed the way he lay or sat or knelt or got up to walk the whole way down the stairs.

But if night is a stairs, it is also the last but one rung of stars. If a fortress unguarded, also our native honey.

It seems I heard the pendulum's last tick a long time ago. Ages ago. As though it came out of childhood, where in my father's house, a clock counted passersby all night, and in the morning, I had to sweep up the strewn minutes from every corner, buttons, needles, and seeds, and no two alike. The last tick was long ago. I'm beginning to suspect I'll have to wait until tomorrow to hear the next. Between the last and the next, I sleep like a seed. Or I lie like a needle my mother fixed to the cloth, to mark the place she left off telling a story. How did it end? Where does that door in the ceiling lead? Will my brother come and wake me soon to say our morning prayers? I remember how we prayed. Stripped to our underpants, we knelt side by side and got on with it. We would fashion our souls to fit the grip of God, so had our work cut out for us. We would be used, would be raised up, good tools, and brought tremendously down, hammers warming in the great hand which uses, hand which giveth and taketh. Who would fashion ourselves thus were earlier than sparrows, though never earlier than our father, who would never have the light find him supine, and who was worn already by years of God's fierce fondling, worn almost to transparency by His use. Sons can only hope to be so used, pray to be so terribly singled out as that one who came before us, inhabited the earth before us, so that the world was unimaginable without him, and now the dwelling places of the soul, as well. Should both or either of us boys arrive at those hallowed reaches, we would expect to find our predecessor and

t
h
e

w
i
n
g
e
d

s
e
e
d

better already there, preparing the ground for us, setting a table to include us. And our sincerest wish was, I know now, too late, not, in fact, to be acknowledged by God, but to be seen, truly seen, seen once and forever, by our father, Ba, who was earlier than light and later than the last each night, whose bloody God exacted love exactly at the body, leveled the force of his divine affection precisely at the fatty heart and fibrous lungs; the wild, old, hairy God wracked Ba's body to instruct Ba's spirit. And Ba got on with it, the labor with texts and thighbones, faith and torso, secrets and pain, numina and heartbreak; he got on with the fashioning. So did we, his sons, in order that we might be seen by him, in order that we might inhabit a room in our father's eyes, one small chamber in his black irises. It was, then, for love, that we got on with it; for love of him who was remote and feared, that we fashioned ourselves, we hoped, into vessels fit for the Holy Spirit to inhabit. We devoted ourselves to the progress of one another's souls. We hammered each other, risked dispersion into a shower of sparks and bright nails, in order to possibly transform ourselves into whole tense sheets of sheer curtain, metal so fine the Lord's light and logos could arrive through us unimpeded. So we got on with it. And though it didn't begin with pain, its end was pain, our delicious affliction. Its end was the strain and numbness our almost naked bodies could endure in long periods of static genuflection, summer and winter. It began with my brother Go and me praying just ten minutes each morning by our beds before leaving for school. I don't remember what moved us to that final prostration, hands and heads to the cold wood floor. With what were we so overcome? What threw us down into that attitude? And did one of us, unsated by ten slim minutes, crave the full meaning of an hour? And then hours? Did the other simply follow? Or did we strive with one another, continually overreaching each other? We strove as lovers strive. We discovered the satisfying roundness of the clock, and began waking earlier, then earlier, moving deeper backward into dark and the previous night, both of us urging ourselves and each other, striving past the first hour, and then the second, and then beyond. And in fact, we weren't striving at all, but remaining in the separate closets of our prayers.

WHAT DID MY father mean when he said *Remembrance?* I remember I was born in the City of Victory on a street called Jilan Industri, where each morning the man selling sticky rice cakes goes by pushing his cart, his little steamer whistling, and by noon the lychee man passes, his head in a rag, bundles of the fruit strung on the pole slung on his neck, while at his waist, at the end of a string, a little brass bell shivers into a fine and steady seizure. I remember I was named twice, once at my birth, and once again after my father, in his prison cell, dreamed each night the same dream, in which the sun appeared to him as a blazing house, wherein dwelt a seed, black, new, dimly human. And so one morning, at a white metal table in the visiting yard, he and my mother decided my name, which, said one way, indicates the builded light of the pearl, and said another, the sun.

It was 1959, the year of the pig, eighteen months after I was born, that my father was arrested by the military police working under President Sukarno, because of things he'd been saying to a handful of men and women who came down every evening to the banks of the Solo River to wash their rice, or beat their clothes clean on the stones, or shit behind the makeshift rattan screens. He'd been warned several times before his arrest that what he talked about those evenings, sitting beside the Solo, might be considered seditious. When he didn't stop, the Indonesian War Administration accused him of being a spy, and threw him in prison for nineteen months. But what could a person say about night and seeds, for it was night and seeds my father talked about, that might so offend a military regime? What is a seed? My son's fourth-grade textbook says something about monocots and dicots. Is it monocot or dicot seeds dictators fear? What was so dangerous about the letters he wrote to my mother and had smuggled out of jail that she had to burn them immediately after she read them? What does a seed enclose that might be considered dangerous to anyone? What was it my father said, standing at evening by the Solo?

Did he say seed planted deep at one sill declares a new house at a further turn of the sun?

Did he say seed is good news, our waiting done?

Did he say seed is told, kept cold, scored with a pocketknife, and then left out to die, in order to come into a further seed, speaking the father seed, leading to seed, if seed can be said to lead, a road we sow ahead of our arrival?

What did he say? Think.

Once upon a time, a seed went walking down a spiral stair, having gotten it in his head he wanted to become a rice. *When,* he wondered, *will I lie down a seed only, a lone stone, and wake up an assembly that feeds, a great rice?* He wanted to feed. *Seed dies,* he thought, *but rice never sleeps, rice is unvanquished.* So he went walking, and asking, *Are you my father?* and *Are you my mother?* of a door, a mirror, and a kitchen knife. The door pinched him, the mirror declared nothing the seed recognized, and the kitchen knife said, *Good night.*

What? asked the seed. *Did you say something?*

Toll, whispered the knife.

Toll? asked the seed.

Pay the toll. You must reckon with your passage.

I have no money, said the seed.

Then I kill you now, whispered the knife. The seed shuddered, and a very thin layer of skin sloughed off.

Wait, he said, *I can give you a riddle.*

A riddle? asked the blade.

I'm good at riddling. I'm a seed.

The blade considered. *Alright,* he said, *but I'm not bad at riddling myself. So tell a riddle I can't unriddle, or you don't pass. No, tell me three.*

The seed thought hard. His first riddle was this:

What an unlikely hand, the wing. What weird feet, claws. What fine math, a nest. What a strange bird, the ear that speaks a flower. It's nearly an open eye. How dark the ore that lies awake all night. And what an unlikely miner, the heart who comes, a hand his only lamp. And what an odd compass, a pebble in a shoe, the heel the only comfort. And what a strange mountain, a seed. What an unlikely kingdom. How narrow a house it keeps. So little shelters us. How still the next world lies inside it.

That's easy, whispered the knife, scraping himself against a whetstone. *The answer is: pilgrim. You're down to two.*

The seed thought harder. His second riddle was this:

My foot, a balding paw, would like to be a hand, recalls too well the wolf it is, would like to play a piano, compose a sonata, knot a tie, don a uniform of thirty buttons. The boot is what it dreams. It loves the heel, adores the glove. My wolf despises what it wants to be, my hand. It steps on the hand, would extinguish the seed buried in the valley of the thumb and index, in the girlish wrist, the ticklish palm, for the hand claps and the wolf dances, the fingers count and he leads the path to water, the map drawn on the foot's own ticklish belly, which a man reads by a hand that touches, that loves the wolf that bites.

The knife yawned. *You better do better than that. You'll be dead sooner than you think. The answer is: siblings.*

The seed began to worry. What was he to do? Those were two of his best riddles, and the knife unriddled them without breaking a sweat on his gleaming forehead. Then he told another:

A woman draws twelve animals on the wall. A man counts the eyes and feet and comes up odd. The window common to them says *Today*, and today a man will come. A man but not a man, riding but not sitting, standing but not leaning on a ladder, bone. A man ringing, rung with the twelve secret hips of honey, a signal odor of chrysanthemums, the recipe for snow, and the permanent address of the rose. His kisses seal the crossbar under which the two come and go: once to fetch the water and bring it back, once to fetch the children and bring them home, and one last time to hear the folded note a bird left at the end of their human year, all fire.

The knife was stumped. He suspected a trick. A *trick*, he mumbled, *a trick. You're tricking me.*

No, said the seed. *It's a riddle, and a good one. Now hear another.* With confidence renewed the seed told another:

The woman I love gives half her face to the night. The other half she offers to me and one long window that stands at the end of the longest hall of the house I abandoned in a field of dandelion one day while the seed was blowing and the townspeople pulled down the bell-house and the one-eyed bell, and put up a blind clocktower. Is it my mother's house? Is it my father's? From where come the voices of the children?

The woman I love gives half her face to the night, in which she pauses on a stair to hear the water falling down for miles, and coming from unroofed leagues, and cold, so cold it numbs her mouth and wakes a seed, kissed into flowering.

The knife was almost wild with rage. *This better not be a trick,* he whispered.

Do you need more time? asked the seed, *or shall I assume I've told two which are beyond you? Let me tell my third, then I'll be on my way.* The seed began.

My right hand writes my letters, my left hand smuggles a seed into the ground. My hungry hand blesses. My fat hand reprimands. But my fat worm gets hungry, and though my woman lies unguarded, I ask where's the door? Where the morning glory closes at evening. Which is past the great meadows of cotton gins, and steel mills abandoned to clover and the honeybee, in whose antennae hums a spiral code and bright arithmetic.

Where the morning glory closes at evening, an unfinished house stands. And the house accomplished. There a bird flits between opposite sills, a facing ledge and my own, which I can't see, many dark elbows down and hidden by an eave.

Opposite houses and the one I inhabit is twice-hidden, by light all day, by nearness the long night, when I lean on a jamb to hear a bird call from its unseen sleep. Opposite calls, and one is heard, the one without a destiny, untroubled by the color of your hair, unencumbered of any wish, while unheard goes the very shape of longing, the sum of an unencompassable face, the call without seam or margin, and we face it.

So tell the man whose head is bowed, who's waiting to hear from me, if he looks up he'll see the guests are leaving the feast. Tell him while his one hand inches along the frayed margin of his father's cloth his mother mends,

l
i
.
y
o
u
n
g

l
e
e

the other hand falls to the threshing floor to lie, blind among the blind grain.

But don't tell him my name.

And he who loved me once, who has forgotten me, all of me fallen from him like scales or old thorns, making his journey lighter, tell him his shadow of discarded leagues arrives before him everywhere he goes. And she who had forgotten me, who thinks of me tonight, doubling me by patiently not finding me under her cooking spoon, in either furrow between her eyes, tell her I'm close, the insect counting in her unguarded wrist.

But don't tell either of them my name.

And the boy who would make my picture with his pencil, who draws the lines over and over, multiplying me, his drawing hand growing sore, his paper beginning to tear, tell that one who darkens me, and darkens me, and darkens me, don't cry! The path relinquished finds its way is home by a star's influence. Lift your face from your hands, tell him, and set it toward an indoor sea. See? It becomes what it faces. And the hands, the hands hang. Leave them. Tell him they'll find water. But don't tell him my name.

It's nice riddling with you, but I really must go now. I'm going to be a rice. Then he started walking away, but as he turned to go, the knife, incensed at having been bested, suspicious at having been duped, flew down from the cutting board on which he'd been standing, and struck the seed, killing him on the spot.

But what is a seed? Is it the apple? Is it a Kingdom? To hold a seed, weightless, in the palm of your hand, is to think, *Soon*. If it is a morning glory seed, you hold both the flower and where the flower closes at evening, where another country begins, and double doors open toward us, the seam of their parting widening to vanquish utter margins unto the first day: Noon, a woman is dressing for our journey together, combing her hair opposite the direction of our arrival. Her name appears in ledgers of ships whose masts have long passed out of view, dispelling any rumor of a horizon or setting sun. And soon, the sun, that bell, struck some million years ago, will tell the note it meant. Soon, a seed will wake, who lay all night along a ledge. Meanwhile, I cradle in my hand this odorless seed like one dead, like one who recalls nothing of his actions or inactions, one who bears inside now only a remembered shapeliness of certain desires and needs, no longer recognizable as desire or need, but things more elemental, akin to oceans, sandstorms, and the yearning wings reveal by their action in time. I remember the back gate where I planted morning glory seven years ago. Walking there last fall, I noticed that the vine had dropped all its flowers. But the leaves were intact; green, heart-shaped, they hid the pods that kept the seeds.

A morning glory's seedpods look like miniature sultans' turbans and each is as big as a good-size drop of blood. Shaking them a little, the rattling made me think that each might hold inside it a meticulous clock. Breaking them open, I saw they were merely the gold husk to the blacker thoughts, the seeds! Thought is black! Why does the morning glory have no fruit? What does the flower signal? Each year I must wait past the glory's green polyp, past the bruise-colored bud, and later than the lavender flower, in order to break into the gold pods, pop them between my fingers, and scatter black, news-bearing seeds in a glass dish.

Now, my wife, I have the presiding feeling that you and I might share the same body. Against all reason and rationale, my body feels convinced to its deepest cell it is continuous with the body of you who lie beside me, who in fact lies the length of my body, shoulder to ankle-bone, your hip set inside the bowl of my loins. And yet, at the same time, you remain out of reach, utterly un-reachable, as though you did not lie here at all, but waited for me on the other side of a country only my fly-ing to you names, and names so softly you need not waken to hear my approach, which is the shape of this night.

Love, wake up. Don't sleep. What is the nature of our shared body? What garment could we possibly weave to contain it? Would the garment not be, in fact, the very body, and what we daily make between us? Therefore the stars figure in. A garment not made on any loom of bone and a red shuttle. A dress, this body we share. Yet, what is its shape? Is it a fish? Is it a house? Is it a burning cross, a fountain of fatal birds, clocksprings newly wet in the fire, a nest of punctual seeds, quiver of irrevocable arrows, a clock tower telling the name of the traveler re-ceding unto all four compass points of today? Is it today? What is today? A door swinging four ways in the wind to let go a handful of birds, seeds, a woman asleep in a nest of thorns, a joy deferred? Is it a church? Our shared body is a church, then, and the size of a seed, as any true church must be. So this woman and I are wed at a seed, and I weave a various garment for that seed, a seed garment.

But what is a seed? Something I never read in any book keeps me awake tonight, something my father said. And my father is coming for me. I feel the gravity of his arrival as though my own body drew him from the East, as though even now he tramples the dew in order to step out of the night and hand me a stone I can't bear to refuse, yet must die to receive. What is the question he will surely ask of me? What do I need to know? Close my eyes. If we're very quiet, we can hear the sun. Listen. The nighthawk! I hear the nighthawk!

Its cries unlock our hair. With us all summer, hunting, he makes two sounds. His circling overhead is accompanied by a near-cry, while as he dives he emits a groan, an almost comic O, to remind the listener that any cry he thinks he hears is in himself. The first is the one that scrapes the scalp and tightens a single thread about the heart. The second is a croak. I hear him every night at this hour. He dives and turns to the call his body casts ahead, scoping by sound, sweeping the insect air, to feast on little wings in the dark somewhere. If he combs our hearts, may he not find us random. Nor too determined. Rather, let. The way the sun is let, all those rooms, and for hours, listen. Wind in the leaves, our children in the next room breathing. Listen.

A man who lives among women and children, if I'm

very quiet, mornings, I can sometimes hear, as though out of the vacant future, the voice of a child reading out loud pages turning in another room. And if I'm patient, I can hear the patience in the mother's voice urging softly, *Go on.*

A man who lives among women and children, I can some mornings, if I'm very quiet, hear, as though out of the purchased past, a boy reading out loud to his mother, in a room made quiet by her. In that room, even now, the birds unlisten morning into a blue hearing, prelude to the verdict sun.

But here it is night, and anyone awake this late, weighing for himself seeds and forgetfulness, the white grains of his insomnia and the weight of the whole night, must begin to suspect he is of no particular origin, though sit at a window long enough, late enough, and you may yet hear a secret you'll tomorrow, parallel to the morning, tell on a wide, white bed, to a woman like a sown ledge of wheat. Or you may never tell it, you who lean across the night and miles of the sea, to arrive at a seed, in whose dim house resides a thorn, or a wee man, carving a name on a stone at a fluctuating table of water, the name of the one who has died, the name of the one not born unknown. Someone has died, and someone is not yet born. And while the ink is wet, I write. While the well is black. And the children dream of haunted schoolrooms. As long as someone looks for me, and I go unfound by wand or compass, tendril or seed.

And what was it my father said about the seed? Things my father said I can't completely remember. But the voice he used remains, without enduring. And a festival is foretold by a hidden calendar at the heart of a strong reiterating pip, presently entombed, awaiting breakage, while I sit here holding it, waiting.

I sit here as I did with my sister and brothers when we were children, we who sat very still for our father, while he made drawing after drawing of us in pencil, his hand moving over the paper seemingly on its own, his eyes trained on what he was drawing, us, and not on what he'd drawn. How bored and frustrated I was those days I sat so still for him, and hours at a time. And as his hand moved to make a face or an arm appear on a white tablet which he held propped on his knees below his own face, I could feel large parts of myself being vanquished by his gaze and his drawing hand, as though, being translated that way to rough page and graphite by my father, there would soon remain nothing of me. Or else there would be so little of me, I might eventually appear. For he was making me go away so completely, I was beginning to arrive. And as his hand and eyes realized more and more of me, less and less of me remained. I was nothing but a lump of heavy time expiring, a clay vase going porous, a stone, a seed. I was one of those seeds my father kept in the pocket of his suit which hung in the closet.

I REMEMBER MY father's sermon on the seed, which he told by candlelight, in the church basement in Pennsylvania. It was during the blizzard of 1975. The Women's

Auxiliary sat in a circle around him, sewing blankets. He
leaned across a table and said that the hour had come
for us to put an ear to the seed, to hear the lightning
scratched there, late news of our human spring. Or was
that his sermon on the spring? From my father's sermon
on the trees, I remember only the sound of trees. From
things he said on the falling leaves, I recall a rake left lying in the apple orchard. From what he told about the
seven boats, all I have are ten broken stairs darkening to
the sea. What was it he said about the seed? Only the
seed that hoarded winter to its heart . . .? Only the water
broken into by winter could . . . No. That was his sermon on winter. On that topic he had a lot to say; so
much, in fact, that he devoted a month of Sundays to it,
though I remember only his notion that there were not
many winters in a life, but only one, a fathering winter, a
paternal January and eternal season. That, he claimed, is
the winter we have to outwinter, crucial season of death.
In the face of death's winter, it's best to keep a wintering
heart, detached to its depths, the wider scope of indiffer-
ence. That was his January message, told with alarm in
his otherwise even voice, like a warning I keep in my
head these days when I am the exact age he was when I
was born. His symbol for attachment was the proverbial
house built on sand. Disengagement turns the ground
solid, was what he tried to tell me. I regarded his words
as the natural claim of a man who'd been forced to dis-
engage over and over, having at eight years old lost a sister to rabies, at twelve the nanny who helped birth him
and even fed him her milk, at sixteen a mother to mur-

the winged seed

der, at twenty-five a first son to China, and at thirty a second to meningitis. So if he thought he was warning me, or anyone else, I think he was talking to himself those afternoons. Those afternoons in winter all become one winter afternoon, a room of light scarcely furnished with a ladder-backed chair; a cold, bright, enclosed porch where dry, brittle ivy hung like small bells from stone pots and my father stood talking, while I wrote down what he said. For I was my father's secretary from the time my writing was legible to him, around the age of fourteen. I wrote what my father thought out loud each Friday after school, helped him memorize it all day Saturday, and knew if he spoke or misspoke Sunday morning, when he opened his mouth for the sermon.

He began reciting on Saturdays when the sun was slightly past its zenith, yet bright in the highest ice-tipped branches of all four black trees outside the manse windows. The tree trunks were cast into shade, as half the house was by afternoon, from which depths a child's voice, my brother's, could be heard. He was reading out loud the stories from that great book our father made us read each day and my brother read all day Saturday. I could hear my brother's bored monotone coming from his shut room, while I listened to my father recite, and I read along in silence the typed draft of his previous day's thinking, I wished I could be reading the book my brother was reading.

There were a lot of books in that house. But there was ever only one book: the one my father used to teach me to read. Called by him The World, it was bound by un-

l
i

•

y
o
u
n
g

l
e
e

seen thread and glue, and covered in black leather; the book which, I believed, had no author other than a three-bodied God, a monster in my eyes. The words of the book formed two black columns on white leaves thin as tracing paper. But it was the pictures I thought most about as my father spoke and I waited to correct him.

The pictures in the book were as strange as the stories they illustrated. The beautiful pictures, richly colored, filled my head as I followed my father from room to room, from the study to the screened-in porch, helping him commit his words to his memory, and, inevitably, to mine, even if all I was thinking about were those pictures. Bodies, naked or barely draped in blue robes and red robes; the brown and yellow breasts of old men and young men; the golden shoulders and thighs of thick-limbed women and girls; the fleshy waist of God; his white beard and huge hands; and the pale neck of a virgin mother. But also the other bodies, the shamed attitudes of two naked ones; a murdered brother falling under a red sky; a sacrificial son bound on an altar; a decapitated giant; a blind beggar; a stranger knocking; a crucified thief. There were many pictures. But together they made one picture: my father.

Without fail, like a train on time, each Saturday night, with my father's words ringing in my head, I dreamed of him. Sometimes he said things I felt I had to write down, but couldn't find pencil or paper. Sometimes I followed him as in his black coat he climbed up and down a narrow ladder, saying things I forgot upon waking. Sometimes he sowed a handful of sparrows and seeds across my mother's kitchen table, scattering them, tiny and many, impossible to gather. In a recurring dream, I walk, late and in a hurry, toward my father's church, which shrinks as I approach, becoming soon the size of a dollhouse, and growing smaller and smaller the nearer I come. By the time I reach its red double doors, the church is the size of a walnut, and I have to crawl on my hands and knees to enter. He meets me inside. Sitting with his back against the chancel and his legs hugged to his chest, he smiles, welcoming me. I crimp and hump, twist and tuck my limbs this way and that in order to sit across from him, while he, to make room for me, closes like a fist, pulls himself into a tight fetus until, finally, we are sitting face to face, bony knee to bony knee, burning forehead to wrinkled forehead, sucking the used air. Light from the stained-glass windows, broken up and translated into a various spectrum, falls sallow on our faces. And in this dream, as it was when he was alive, I look down, veering from his black eyes. I was never allowed to look my father straight into his eyes. Only one time did I do that. It was an accident. It was during church service, and I don't know how long he had been staring at me, but by the time I saw him, it was too late, because by then I was looking directly into his eyes. And then there was no turning away. His gaze forbade it. And I wanted nothing more than to look away, to avoid his penetration. Yet I wanted nothing more than to look. I wanted nothing more than for *him* to look away. *I* would penetrate *him*, I thought. So I looked. And looked. What did I see? A formidable head, black eyes, black brows, black mustache. Full, almost sensuous lips. It was the head I'd seen on posters and flyers all over Hong Kong when we lived there and he preached to thousands each week.

It was the head my sister, as a child, had thought she'd seen on the black-and-red posters that covered the walls of the outdoor bazaar in Jakarta, Indonesia. Such images were everywhere on the island, portraits not of our father, but of President Sukarno, whom our father strangely resembled. The size of large windows, they were plastered all over buildings, even the sides of buses. Below one of such posters, I remember, was an overturned pedicab, twisted bicycle frame, folded wheels, shocked spokes, three broken bodies, and a dense swarm of spectators, some standing, others squatting and fanning themselves. Our own cabby had stopped and dismounted to tell a policeman what he saw: an automobile had rammed the pedicab ahead of ours and thrown both the passengers as well as the cabby into the street.

The guilty driver of the automobile was now out of his car and offering cigarettes to the witness and the policeman, pushing unopened packs of cigarettes into the uniformed officer's breast pockets. The officer leaned slightly forward to take between his lips the cigarette that was held to his face, then leaned again to the struck match, his hands the whole time hooked to his belt. By now everyone was talking at once, waving their hands and pointing emphatically, jabbing at this and that other thing. The officer surveyed the scene, smoking in silence, until he spotted someone trying to help one of the victims to her feet. *Put her down!* he yelled. *And put something under her head!*

My mother, my sister, Fei, my brother Go, and I didn't move from our seat in the cab, and our mother, knowing we would be stuck like that a while, opened her purse and began to dispense candy, when Fei said, *Look,* and pointed to a spot on the street. It was a lump of fatty, milk-colored, blood-smirched pudding of some sort. *Brains,* Fei whispered. It could have been anything: the cast-off entrails of a freshly slaughtered pig, or a jellyfish thrown out of a bucket of netted fish. But *Brains,* was what Fei said.

My father was not among us, for he'd been arrested months ago by the military police, and was now in prison awaiting trial. High on a wall was the poster of the man who'd had him arrested: Sukarno, president of the Republic of Indonesia. His huge head set on a thick neck, he seemed to gaze over the commotion of the market, over the roofs of stalls and the heads of shoppers, the tables of meats, and fruits, and cloths, and vegetables, and assorted musical instruments and Moslem paraphernalia, over the traffic of the daily, over the trees, over the River Solo, over the tumult of the present into some other clarity. For he had a look about him of someone whose attention was wholly trained upon a great immanence. The artist of the poster must have been looking up at him when the portrait was made, for the contour of the head with a fez on it, and the massive, medal-bedecked shoulders, resembled nothing so much as an image hewn from a cliff.

While his face was everywhere, our father, on the other hand, was hidden from us, a prisoner in the ruler's palace, so we believed. The palace was surrounded by armored cars, jeeps, and khaki-uniformed, belt-strapped men, wearing buttons and medals and guns. And then, just as suddenly, Fei gasped, *It's Ba! Where?* our mother asked, startled. *It's Ba!* Fei said again, pointing to the poster. And when our mother saw that Fei was pointing at the picture of Sukarno, she broke into tears. We pleaded, *Don't cry, Mu, it's Ba,* while she shook her head, explaining that, no, it wasn't our father. *Have you forgotten what your father looks like?* she asked.

The fact is, by that time, our father seemed a virtual stranger to us, and the hours we spent waiting for him seemed endless. And while our mother's absence from us as she spent all her days at the prison became an emptiness around which our activities circled, it only punctuated that greater absence we called Ba, our father. Though our mother was often absent, Ba was The Absent One. He grew immense as our mother's days and thoughts revolved around his not being there. And though we daily hoped for his release, his absence had begun to feel like a permanence we simply lived with, never doubting it, reliable as gravity, or True North. It became our very world, and as a world, he became less keenly felt, more and more assumed, as though we'd always lived without him, as though he hadn't been taken from us only six months ago, but ages ago. Ba's absence receded from our daily thoughts into abstraction, even while we became its most intimate inhabitants. And this even though we prayed in front of his picture each night.

Each night, our mother repeated for us the story of our father: he was a prisoner, she would try to get him out, we had to pray. By that time, though, our praying had changed. Without our realizing it, the subject of our prayers, Ba, had gradually become the object of our prayers as well, so that we were praying *to* him as well as *for* him. Each night, standing before his photograph, my brother Go and I on either side of our sister, Fei, we prayed, ending, *Dear Ba. Help Ba. We love Ba. Amen.* Judging by the way we prayed, it was up to Ba to get himself out of his absence and restore himself to us.

In those days, we were often visited by groups of three or four soldiers looking for money or sellable goods. So it wasn't a surprise when, one morning, while we were eating breakfast, they came to our door. But refusing to be bought off by cigarettes or money this time, and acting insulted by the bribes they'd often enough accepted, the officer in charge extended a few official apologies, and then gave prompt orders to his underlings to search the house thoroughly. By the time they left, all of Ba's papers, letters, and manuscripts were collected, boxed, and removed. Also taken away were any pictures we had of him, including the photograph on the little black table we prayed to each night. During the ransack Sheeti and Lammi, our nannies, cried, *Give us Dwan's pictures! Let the children have their father's images!* while our mother stood wooden, silent, all trace of feeling seemingly erased from her.

Yet we continued to perform our nightly ritual in front of the empty table that had previously held his photo. Our mother instructed us to fix in our minds a clear image of Ba's face before we began to pray. Standing before the table and the absent photograph, we all three closed our eyes to see his face, and then uttered our supplications for the man called Ba, to the power called Ba. But the image was no longer vivid. We were beginning to lose the subject of our prayers. With it, we were losing the object. Our endeavor grew vaguer and vaguer.

Years after that incident, though, I was looking into my father's eyes. And I knew what his look meant. It meant, *I see you clean through.* And I could not look away. So there we were that day, me standing in blue among the choir, listening to a woman perform her solo before the rest of us joined in refrain, and my father, seated behind the pulpit, stilled, robed, looking like a fluted black monument. And I knew that the body he covered from neck to midcalf was scaly and rough, practically sloughing off when he scratched and scraped it, itchy, with a silver kitchen knife. And I knew that pinned to him beneath his robe and black mantle was the red rosebud I'd given him that morning, wilting, shot through by the needle, pressed between a heavy weave and my father's wild heart.

While the soloist urged, *Come to the mercy seat,* and *Come to the seat of love,* to the congregation, men, women, children, sleepers, believers, rich, poor, every hair of every head numbered, I stared straight into my father's eyes, and within seconds was no longer looking, only stubbornly locked, gaze and gaze with him, my black irises to my father's.

I would lose. I had to. I could not sustain it. Against my every will and command, my eyes, betrayers that they are, deserters that they are, looked down, my face burning with . . . what? Shame? Anger? Fear? Could he see what was burning my cheek? Was my rose staining his lapel?

I was seventeen, and I had seen that look on my father's face numerous times. There was sternness in it, but it was more than sternness. There was even something predatory about it, though it went beyond anything merely animal. It was my father possessed. But in my dream of the little church, he cups his hands as though he's gathered something to show me. I lean forward and look down into his hands. Two trees. He shows me two bonsai trees. It is some sort of miracle, and I am moved to the beginnings of terror by the intensity, the reality, of what I'm seeing: a miniature tree growing out of each of his palms, and encircling the base of each trunk is a slim ring of blood. The branches of the trees are tangled, the gnarled thorny limbs of the left-hand tree braided with the black, flower-laden branches of the right-hand tree. *It is so real*, I say, and suddenly have the sensation that something has been revealed to me, that what he shows me explains everything between us. He speaks, or I hear the words out of nowhere: *According to how you sow, for thorn or flower* . . . then the voice falters, and I wake, but not before I notice we are wearing the same shoes.

I REMEMBER NOW, in his sermon on the shoes, my father exhorted the listener to build a shoe fit for a word to
don and strike its way over earth. Make a shoe for a traveler word, he'd said while he was alive, a shoe for walking
over the dead, lying end to end. Corpses and a great, terrible day must not keep each from walking beside words
or rectitude of heart. And we must forgive a word's lame-
ness, for it was meant to be at sea, and the price of rest
inside the shoe moving over the earth was hobbling.

On communion Sundays, I went with him after
morning service on his rounds through the river valley.
We performed the ritual eating with those of his congregation who were "shut-ins," those who never left their
houses, mainly old, infirm, crazy, or dying. In town, they
lived in cramped rented rooms that smelled of boiled
vegetables, moldy carpeting, and musty couch cushions.
Outside of town, they were the ones inhabiting broken-
shingled low houses set a few feet from the road, sometimes in a field alone or next to a rotten shed or the
hulks of abandoned cars. Many of them were the same
people I delivered food to once a week as a volunteer for
Meals-on-Wheels, riding with two men sixty years old,
an ex–coal miner and a security guard at the steel mill,
in a station wagon carrying hot dinners to shut-ins.

While my father drove, I kept my hand on the square,
black leather case between us. With a handle on the top,
it bore one shiny clasp in the front which, undone, freed

the lid and let the bifold front open outward, revealing inside the blue velvet interior and four small wooden tiers, each holding five brightly polished communion glasses no bigger than shot glasses.

We headed out after lunch, around one o'clock, and with luck we'd be able to make six visits. My father would have liked to do more in one day, but we couldn't plan on it, since the visits sometimes dragged, the shut-ins eager to keep in their chairs any infrequent guest. With that, and the time on the road in between, we usually got home no sooner than ten o'clock. For me it was a trial, and my favorite time was in the car on the road. We passed hills and pastures, snowy for miles, and watched the white day go gray. Trees stood like old gates on white knolls, and if the weather were warm a few days in a row, black creeks appeared in gullies and blue ravines. We saw deer at the edge of trees, and drove over furry, wind-riffled carcasses of raccoons and groundhogs. Sometimes the sky turned to snow and we slowed on blind descents.

The road out of town, a two-lane black macadam, wound past a whole hillside of graves. One spring, a heavy rain washed half the hill down onto the road along with a few of the buried inhabitants. Each time we drove by the cemetery, I looked up at the one monument which only I knew my father was thinking of when one Sunday he preached, saying: *The knight on the grave of a rich man weighs less upon sons than a father who requires walking on waves, buoyancy in time!* We drove along the graveyard's iron fence until we turned the bend and saw the huge back of the sign which we knew read *Welcome to Vandergrift*. Already I was sleepy and bored, but happy to be sitting next to my silent father. Some silences between us were tense, perennial tests. But my father's silences on Sunday afternoons, after the morning of preaching and public prayer, were relaxed and easy on both of us.

On Sundays, if we weren't making rounds, we were at home observing silence. At least twice a week, our family kept a whole afternoon of quiet, neither speaking nor whispering, my father, my mother, my sister, three brothers, and I keeping everything to ourselves in the one house of three floors of square rooms and identical doors. It was clarifying, the quiet, and our stillness felt like a deep liberty. It was one more detail of my life with my father which made me feel strange in a world which found my family strange, with our accented speech and permanent bewilderment at meatloaf.

In the car, the heater hummed and I read the list of names my father had written out earlier. We'd make the rural visits first, and start working our way back toward Vandergrift around six o'clock. By then, the sun would have already fallen and our ride grown darker by hours. We'd be heading into town from the other end, opposite the way we left, and my father, as was his habit, would choose roads unlit except by car headlights, in order to drive past an old brewery and the fenced grounds of the shut-down foundries, the steel mills half manned, and through empty downtowns of places called Truxall, Moween, Tintown, New Kensington, and Apollo, my father and I tired by then and him humming as we passed streets named for trees, Maple, Elm, and Oak, or Grant, Sherman, and Polk, the names of the dead.

But our last rural stop was Ethel Black's place. A few yards down the road from a truckers' bar, her house sat behind dense trees and next to a ditch exposing a clay pipe. The ruts were deep and icy in the driveway that wound right up to the back door. By now I was hungry, impatient, my feet freezing, and my trouser legs damp. My father smiled at me and said, "One more visit, in town, after this, then we'll have done a little good." A glum fourteen, I was not cheered.

The dilapidated house had a sagging back porch and buckled aluminum siding. A silver Christmas tree from two years ago leaned against the porch railing, the brown nest in its arms abandoned. Seeds were scattered for birds among stacks of newspapers, miscellaneous junk, a vacuum cleaner, some paint cans and loose bureau drawers. Mouse and rabbit droppings were all over boxes and a black pot sprouted some frozen yellow grass. We huffed through the wreckage, my father ahead, and me balancing in both hands the blood and fresh corpse of The Resurrected Man, as my father was fond of calling the one whose body we'd been swallowing all afternoon.

Beside a rickety utility shelf of dead potted daisies, the kitchen windowpane was broken and mended with duct tape and cardboard. My father rapped at the back door and walked in calling, "Mrs. Black?" Getting no answer, he raised his voice again, "Mrs. Black?" We walked

through the cramped dingy kitchen lit by the illuminated clock over the stove. The place smelled of rotting
garbage and my father pointed to bags of it in the corner,
reminding me to take them out with us when we left. A
mound of shit sat reeking on a newspaper in the rusty
sink with a trickling faucet. The kitchen was a loosely
heaped firetrap of blown-out pilots and fuses and hundreds of days of newspapers stacked on the stove and
tabletop. The counters were cluttered with varying sizes
of colored glass paperweights Ethel Black collected before she fell down and broke her hip ten years ago.
Everywhere were ashtrays heaped with ashes and butts
smoked by a fat, thirty-year-old, mentally handicapped
"case" from the special education program who, trained
as a geriatric aide, came as a visiting nurse twice a week
to Ethel's house, and sat in the kitchen and listened to
her transistor radio. It was a case of the helpless helping
the worse off, the variously abandoned in their like
abandonment.

The living-room curtains were drawn and an antique
floor lamp glowed dimly in a corner with a crocheted
shawl thrown over the dirty shade. And there on the sagging ruin of a green-and-yellow couch lay the frighteningly little bag of bones which was Ethel Black. Toothless,
gape-mouthed, and bug-eyed, her head was thrown back
and she stared at the ceiling as if at God, and you couldn't
tell she wasn't a corpse until you heard her wheeze or she
smacked her lips to wet them. Mrs. Ethel Black was in this
condition for as long as I knew her. Sometimes she spit up
sour-smelling water, on bad days she mumbled, "Help me.

Help me. Help me," until you were ready to cry or scream, unless you learned to not listen. There was no other way but the latter if I would follow my father through house after house of similar suffering, room after room of a dying congregation.

Half hag, half child, half awake or asleep, she was wrapped up to the chin in six or seven tattered, gaudy-colored afghans. I sometimes wondered if she was conscious enough to even wish she were better off, wish she might be as lucky as Bernie Flick up the road. "At least Bernie can sit up," Constance the nurse has said, and it's true I've seen him sitting and talking to himself on his bed, which his children, all grown and with litters of kids, moved into the kitchen so Bernie could be in arm's reach of the refrigerator. Bernie slept by an oven, and had bad dandruff.

Mrs. Black's hair was a yellowish gray, as if she might have been blonde once, and she kept it in a long thick dry braid tied at the end with strands of different-colored yarn. It was strange to see such a decrepit body with so much hair. She squirmed a little under layers of musty quilt. I later found out her hands were tied to her body to prevent her from scratching herself, a nervous condition the otherwise rigid eighty-six-year-old lady had which left her skin open, raw, and infected. Looking at her, I heard my father's voice say, "Our god is surely an ironic god," though I knew it was all in my head, what I wished he would sometimes say, so I wouldn't be the only one thinking it.

When I was a boy I made, as children are apt to do,

lists of everything, from names of islands to kinds of stars, Java to roses, which I mistook for stars, "the ones that don't shine in the night garden," from an old Chinese lyric my mother favored. I made lists of cars, chapters-by-heart, and lists of things my father never said to me, which included "Put 'er there, Son," and "Faith is all peril, every hour."

Nevertheless, I knew he thought it, what he'd never admit to me. And I see now his faith in his God was learning to winter-out those Pennsylvania winters and those hard communions. But if those communions were difficult, were they empty? was my continual question. Was my father wasting his time? Was he wasting his life? How was I supposed to feel about it? Even now, I feel either communion happened in that room, or my memories are crushed chalk to my tongue.

When my father preached between 1963 and 1964, on the island of Hong Kong, he drew crowds in such numbers that rows of folding chairs had to be set up in the very lobbies of the theaters where his revival meetings took place, while loudspeakers were set up outside, where throngs of sweating believers stood for hours in the sun, listening to him speak and pray.

Once, while my sister and I were buying sugarcane from our favorite street vendor, the afternoon suddenly filled with red and blue leaflets dropped from an airplane. My sister snatched one out of the air and the two of us looked at a picture of our father, under which was printed, in Chinese and English, the words *Your Friend*, and then the time and place of the next meeting of the

Ling Liang Assembly and Ambassadors for Christ. I recognized the photograph as the same one my mother had taken of our father a little over a year ago on the boat from Indonesia to Hong Kong. His profile, taken by the camera from a lower angle, was backed by the sky and mast, perfect for the image of a helmsman or captain of souls. Only his family knew that when the photo was taken, we were on the way to a detention center. My father and his family were being shipped from one prison in Jakarta to another on some remote island, where, so we were told, we would be given a house and yard which we would not be permitted to leave. But on the way there, a former student of his from Gamaliel University pulled up alongside the ship with a smaller boat, so my parents assembled us in the night, and one stood above the other and handed to the one below, by hoisting over a railing, one by one, each of their five children. The two boats, big and small, rocked unevenly, the gap between them closing and widening, yet less dangerous than a guard asleep somewhere, or else awake but turned away to earn my father's bribe. By the next morning we were in the home of a congregation member of the Ling Liang Assembly. It was during one of the evening revival meetings, when members from the congregation gave personal testimonies of the working hand of God, that my father, convinced we had escaped harm due to some miracle and for some higher purpose, recounted the horrors of the last three years fleeing Sukarno and our rescue. Within a year of that testimony, he was performing mass baptisms in the ocean at night. Hundreds gathered once a month on the beach to watch my father take off his silk suit jacket, his narrow leather shoes and silk socks, roll up his sleeves and wade out into the dark water, from where we could hear him beckoning, *Come! Come to me, come farther, don't be afraid.* And one by one he embraced them and plunged them backward into the surf.

Many years later in the United States, and nearly five years after my father had died, I was eating with my family in a Chinese restaurant in the South Side of Chicago when we discovered through a friendly conversation with the proprietor that he and his wife had been great fans of my father, and had left the Ambassadors for Christ after my father left Hong Kong. The man recollected our father's first testimony and remembered sermons he found particularly memorable. He recounted to us our own story as though it were someone else's: the narrow escape, the faked names, the path to freedom and God. I was filled with a mixture of sadness and disgust, even shame. He sat with us and drank cup after cup of green tea, he and my mother weeping.

Why did I feel disgust? The facts were plain enough, and my father told them plainly, and the man remembered them accurately, to all of our astonishment. And it didn't bother me much that my father or this man attributed so much to a divine hand. I too believe that we are, all of us, for the most part, carried by something beyond us. And though I'd argue emphatically about this or that aspect of God with my father, that wasn't what bothered me when I heard that man in the restaurant talk, good man that he was, kind that he was, a fellow immigrant, as lost in America as we were. Part of me felt such confusion and anger I was almost ready to disavow everything. Why? What makes a person want to disavow his own life? What did I feel so uneasy about? What was it I felt I needed to tell that man? What little detail did I need to give him, to explain he'd got it all wrong? What irked me? Why don't my shoes fit?

When I was six and learning to speak English, I talked with an accent anyone could hear, and I noticed early on that all accents were not heard alike by the dominant population of American English speakers. Instead, each foreigner's spoken English, determined by a mother tongue, each person's noise, fell on a coloring ear, which bent the listener's eye and, consequently, the speaker's countenance; it was a kind of narrowing, and unconscious on the part of the listener, who listens in judgment, judging the speaker even before the meaning or its soundness were attended to. While some sounds were tolerated, some even granting the speaker a certain status in the instances of, say, French or British, other inflections condemned one to immediate alien, as though our gods were toys, our names disheveled silverware, and the gamelan just gonging backward. And I could clearly hear each time I opened my mouth the discord there, the wrong sounds, the strange, unmanageable sharps and flats of my vowels and my chewed-up consonants. What an uncomely noise. More than once I was told I sounded ugly. My mouth was a shame to me, an indecent trench. A recurring dream of mine as a boy who'd just arrived on the continent with my parents was my mouth full of rotten teeth, hundreds of teeth in my mouth and all of them cavity-ridden, brown, chips of burnt bone embedded in my gums. I still remember the feeling of being asked a question in English and, after a brief moment of panic, starting to move my lips, contort my tongue to make the sounds, and opening my mouth nervously to answer, too shy to move my hands to help and make the point, only hoping I made sense to my American listeners, teacher or schoolmate, who were sometimes patient, but whose ears were more often so baffled by my confounded din, they winced in annoyance and asked, *What did you say?* or, turning to someone else in complete exasperation, *What did he say?*

I'm thinking of that now because my sons have just made a new friend, a Chinese boy, seven years old, who lives two houses up the street with his parents, uncles, aunts, cousins, and a grandmother, much the same way we live. I speak to him in Mandarin, but he tells me he doesn't speak Chinese, which I take to mean he doesn't speak the same dialect as me. He says this in English and as he speaks, as he struggles to make the very sounds, lowering his head and mumbling like a whipped boy, fingering his lower lip, I am suddenly returned to my own early attempts at making American sounds, and I remember my own deliberate slurring and mumbling in order to hide my mouth, to make my accent less discernible. I want to move my mouth with his, and I don't know if I want to tell him, *Don't worry, the accent wears off, no one will know you're an alien then,* or tell him how

I sometimes miss my own sound. I remember how I used to hold a hand very casually over my mouth when I talked, hoping to hide the alien thing. And I grew to hate its ugliness more than anyone. It hurt my ear and I avoided as much as possible any contact with native English speakers. In their company, I said as little as possible, and over the years made no friends who didn't come from the apartments across the alley from us in East Liberty, Pennsylvania. Large families lived there, people like us, foreigners, and most of the men, like my father, were students at the Pittsburgh Theological Seminary, behind whose parking lot we lived in a big, old, falling-down, drafty, and, to my mind, beautiful house. From India, Hong Kong, Rhodesia, Chile, Taiwan, and Mexico, our neighbors' versions of English were as strangely inflected and accented as our own. The result was that while in Chinese, with my family, I rattled like any good loose child about anything at all, and spoke my broken English without embarrassment with the children on Hoevler Street, in public school or any other place where fluent English was current, I was dumb. Perceived as feeble-minded, I was, like my siblings, spoken to very loudly, as though the problem were deafness. But I was happy, content to talk to no one outside of the world defined by one alley and an empty lot of dirt where my sister and brothers, Fei, Go, and Be, and I played with the others called Raja, Baba, Yijan, and Gee, in every season, from 1964 until our father graduated three years later.

In Mrs. Black's house we kept our coats on. The room

was cold. Ice formed on the glass of the paper-stuffed windows, and a stiff draft came from the chilly hallway. My father picked up from the floor a rough-knitted cap which must have slipped off the old lady. He gently slipped it back over her head.

"Hello, Mrs. Black," he said very loudly, for she was hard of hearing.

"Huh?" the woman answered.

"Good afternoon, Mrs. Black," my father said, leaning close to her ear. "We're here to give you your communion." Then he told me to get two chairs from the kitchen and we set them up next to her couch.

She smelled terrible, had obviously soiled herself, and was half crazed, mumbling about fire under her bed or someone stealing her money. She was completely unaware of what my father and I were doing there. We could have come to rob her, which happened to many old people like her. She seemed vaguely to remember me, so I leaned over to her and called out, "Mrs. Black? Remember me? I was here yesterday."

A look came over her of complete wonder. "You remember me, boy?" she rasped. She spoke her words loud and every word with equal emphasis, so that her phrases sounded robotlike to me, or like chanting, rather than regular speech. The words didn't sound spoken to anyone.

I said, "I'm Reverend Lee's son. Remember? I was here yesterday. We talked. I came with Harry Porter. Remember? Harry says hello, says he'll be out this week to read to you."

"Is it time to go?" she asked, and then, "Who? You read to me? Is it time to go? Shoes. Where are my shoes?"

"Not this minute, Mrs. Black. We'll have communion together first."

"You read to me?" she asked, turning to my father.

"Yes, Mrs. Black, we'll read."

"Pray for me, Parson," she said.

"I pray for you each day, Mrs. Black. You are in my prayers."

"Pray for me, Parson," she repeated in exactly the same tone.

I had just been there yesterday to deliver her evening meal. Untouched, the tray sat where I left it yesterday on the television. Constance was supposed to come and feed her shortly after I left. Either she had not come, or Mrs. Black had refused to eat. My father told me to examine the tray to see if it looked as if the plastic wrap had even been opened. It had not. He made a note and I knew he would have to telephone the visiting nurse service which Mrs. Black's children, who lived far away, were paying for. He would also have to find a member of the congregation who could give up time to visit Mrs. Black to make sure she was getting her basic needs met until a reliable nurse could be found.

I opened the leather box, poured the grape, and my father broke a saltine cracker in a silver plate, said blessings, and laid a piece of the broken cracker in Mrs. Black's mouth, and very carefully held the glass thimble of dark juice to her lips and slowly poured. Then he blessed our portions, which he and I consumed in silence, and blessed our small cups, which we drained. In the car, my father drove and I read the list of names of the people we had seen and the ones we had yet to see. We would not be able to visit all of them today. After one more visit in town, the rest would have to wait until tomorrow for their communion. All of them were the "other" members of my father's congregation, the ones no one ever saw, who couldn't attend services or any of the social functions held at church. Though their names were on the registry, though they were counted, they mostly lived uncounted, discarded lives. Their existence always seemed tangential to other lives. Mrs. Black, for instance, had six children and countless grandchildren, but none of them could get along or even live in the same county without one stabbing another or beating his kin with a lead pipe. So the old woman was left in the charge of a distant cousin, who handed her over to a friend's daughter, who in exchange for room and board nursed her, only to later abandon the old lady.

OUR LIST ALSO included people like Mona Cook, who one very late night showed up in the church waving a knife. That night, my father and I entered his church to-gether and walked down the aisle toward the dim figure of a woman sitting in the front pew. Her back was to us, and she was moaning, *I see the lamb!* over and over, her voice menacing the otherwise still space, a vast nave of cold candles and one book, closed. She had telephoned the manse a few minutes earlier, and had spoken to my father. She needed him, she had cried. *Now!* she had insisted. I could hear her voice, frantic, broken, hysterical, pleading, coming from the black receiver in my father's hand. She was calling from the church.

My father spoke very softly and patiently, addressing her the way he would any of his congregation, with great formality, but a genuine kindness. He used to lie awake at night thinking about them, his prayers worrying God about this or that person's misfortune or pain. I think he loved each and every one of them, and more than I ever felt they deserved, they who referred to him as their heathen minister, these alcoholic mothers (Mrs. Cook was one of those), delinquent children, shell-shocked bus drivers, pedophilic schoolteachers, adulterous barmaids, desiccated widowers, bruised prostitutes (Mrs. Cook was one of those too), boring executives, retarded janitors, liars, cheaters, drinkers, dopers, motherfuckers, prodigals, sinners each and every one of us, and believers. Perhaps it was my father's calling to love every mangled or lost or refused soul.

As I was growing up in my father's house, it seemed to me that his entire life was divided between composing sermons and praying for or ministering to the bodies and souls of the members of that church situated on a hill overlooking the muddy yellow Kiskiminetas River, on whose banks thrived the little wooden houses in the valley, the churches, their Saturday Bingo signs, the tidy backyards, the whitewashed truck tires sprouting pansies and marigolds, the gardens bearing tomatoes, beans, and green onions, while laundry hung in the foundry air. A railroad track ran along the river, and together they carved a deep sign in the valley, one of them conveying trains that hauled steel coils and tractors, the other floating lost baby dolls, condoms, turds, industrial spillage, one uprooted tree with a possum clinging in its branches, bottles, broken lawn chairs, as well as salamanders, hellbenders, dogs, and bottom-feeding fish. From my bedroom window I could look the whole way down into the valley. At night I heard the trains passing. On one side of the valley were the scrap yards, lot after lot of junked cars and wild forsythia, fenced acres of weeds and dismembered iron, steel, and chrome. That hillside gleamed on sunny Sundays, and looked scabbed and rust-scribbled when clouds gathered over the worshiping valley. On the opposite side was the foundry and its system of ladders and chutes and sheds that housed the forges. It was a fact everyone in the village knew that some days, a two-pound tool could slip a workman's selflove grip and drop through fifty feet of cauldron-heated air to hit the cement, ringing the very teeth and hair of each near man and the naked ears of their women blocks away, who, looking up from their work in a kitchen, knew they heard the tool.

It was on that hill my father prayed each night and morning for someone's hip replacement, someone's heart attack, someone's cancer, a tumor, or skin lesions, someone's near-fatal injury at a mining accident, or someone's body burned at the mill, someone's loneliness in a nursing home, someone's runaway daughter, some-

the winged seed

one's criminal son sentenced to death, someone's death, someone's funeral, someone else's funeral. There was so much dying going on in my father's beautiful riverside Pennsylvania town that it was a mystery the pews were so full every Sunday. He said it was precisely because of the dying that one could count eleven churches while standing at one intersection.

Go sit down in the sanctuary, he commanded Mrs. Cook very gently on the telephone. *I'm on my way.* And then he called an ambulance. Mrs. Cook was diagnosed as mad years ago and had spent almost three years languishing in a squalid county hospital. In the meantime, her two teenage daughters fended for themselves, had two abortions apiece, and eventually moved away. When their mother was released after having been supposedly cured, she returned to an empty house.

And now Mona Cook was seeing the lamb! *There's blood on the lamb!* she was yelling, her words broken occasionally by sobs and loud wails. About ten feet away from her my father told me to stand and watch while he walked on. The woman became aware of us and turned. She was gripping a huge kitchen knife. Her face was a frightful mask, cheeks sunken, eyes caved in, mouth turned down in a comic frown, greasy blonde hair tangled and stuck to her tear-soaked face. She was trembling violently as she stepped into the aisle and stood facing my father.

Mona, he said very softly, slowing his long strides. And again, this time nearly querying, *Mona? Can you hear me? Put the knife down, Mona. I'm here now. I'll try to help you, Mona.* He repeated her name and not only repeated it, but said it each time with something in his voice like . . . love. Love was the meaning in his voice. *Mona,* my father called softly. *Put the knife down.* But the claw of her hand held the knife close to her, between her breasts, the point nearly nicking her chin as she shook. *The lamb,* she whimpered, *The lamb. I see the lamb and there's blood all over his body.* By the time the ambulance arrived, she was asleep on one of the pews while my father and I stood watching.

On our list was also the Tucker couple, Andy and Myrtle. Andy was over seventy, Myrtle ten years younger, and they lived by the abandoned train station in an apartment with Andy's granddaughter, Cheryl, a classmate of mine. Cheryl had no parents and no other relatives. In fact, Andy and Myrtle, who were not married, were not actually relatives of Cheryl. They had been friends of her parents, and later adopted the girl and gave her Andy's last name. I don't know how legal any of it was, but Cheryl Bowser went by the name of Cheryl Tucker and called the old man "Grampa" and the old woman, who wore a hat made out of Budweiser beer cans, Myrtle. The girl could be seen hitching rides into other towns on weekends. She was frequently arrested in Pittsburgh for prostitution. One day Andy gave her money and a grocery list and Cheryl telephoned a week later from Florida to say she was living with a man who, it turned out, was old enough to be her father. The last news I heard of her was she was stabbed in the back while hitchhiking her way back to Vandergrift.

I remember now it was Cheryl who asked me in sixth grade one day, *Is it true what they say about you?*

What do they say? I asked, expecting the worst.

They say your house is always dark like no one lives there. So? I shrugged. I'd heard worse.

They say your mother can't speak good English and writes letters all day to a son she threw away in China twenty years ago. Is that true?

So? I said. I'd heard worse.

They say all you people have the same first and last names and your mother can't tell you apart. They say your house is always dark and you play funny music at night.

I wondered if she was going to mention anything I hadn't already heard.

They say you keep snakes and grasshoppers in a bushel on your back porch and eat them. They say you don't have manners, you lift your plates to your mouths and push the food in with sticks. Have you heard what they're saying? Is it true you all sleep in one bed together? And that you have cousins hiding in the basement? That you got kicked out of your country because they didn't want you so now you're here? They say your dad was in jail. They say you don't believe in God, but you worship the Devil.

I wonder, I said, *if the people who told you those things were the same people who told me you don't know who your father is,* after which remark, Cheryl chased me the whole way home, threatening to stab me with her lead pencil.

On our list was also Charlie November, retarded, sixty, whose one-room shack on the hillside was near a turkey farm. One after another, these were the lives we visited. And every hovel was a sad shell that bore an intimate human smell, smells of living and of waste.

In the car, we drove over black roads flanked by white fields and hills, my father wearing the same black cashmere coat he wore on the boat from China to Java, and from Java to Hong Kong, all of us sitting in the third-class hold while the Americans and the British passed over our heads, holding perfumed handkerchiefs to their noses because of the smelly diapers and cans of salty fish. It was the black coat he wore while standing as the token Chinaman at the Seattle World's Fair, shaking hands at the China exhibit. My father was that single black garment, woven of nails and rain, his face the only window, and which I was never allowed to look straight into. As a boy, I called him The Man in the Chimney whenever he put on that coat. When he died, his face was closed to me forever. These days, his face has become a small glass pane at the end of the world, like one of those high windows in the ceiling of Union Station, each the size of my thumbnail. On the station floor are the human shadows, and in the air an anonymous voice is announcing departures and arrivals, and warning everyone *Beware! Man trafficking in seeds.* The seed trade is a dark habit. Is there a doctor I might consult to help me with the shadows? Is there an authority who might help me? What should I do about those windows that make up the arched ceiling of Union Station, where we have arrived? I must be seven years old, standing with my mother, my sister Fei, and my brothers Go and Be, under the American daylight pouring down from a hundred windows. There must be a clock somewhere, outside the ken of my memory, and there must be a calendar, though I can't say for sure. What should I do with our luggage, those suitcases bound in string? What should I do with my father's brushes and pens and pencils and sketchbooks and dictionaries and books I can't read? What must I do about my mother's dresses, and the black cooking pot we carried through seven countries? So little of what I recall is clear or lit, so few faces correspond to voices. Entire days, even years, stand like ruins which permit no clue as to what once stood, and to try to enter those precincts is to cast myself down unlit avenues, where here half of a face appears, and there a voice comes out of a mouth, and up ahead the living and the dead are eating impossibly at the same table. It's mathematical, distance and time add up to shadow. I wasn't born dark. I grew darker by amassing shadows and seeds. Each memory I own is like a photo being eaten away from the edges toward the center, so that first to disappear are any details of place, clues to where someone is standing or sitting, and along with those details goes the reason I should even possess this or that particular memory at all. I have in my mind vivid recollections of persons to whom I can attach no apparent significance, or even a name. But the seed trade doesn't stop there, for entire faces are wiped out. Then the only thing left is a peculiar nod of a head, a certain shrug of the shoulder suggesting a whole personality, a certain slope of a neck. But who are they? To whom do these intimate gestures belong? And it turns out that these pieces are infinitely heavier than any memory I could fabricate. Who is it leading me through a graveyard and pointing out names? Who is it humpbacked and gnarled, putting a finger to her lip to hush me? And who is the girl I see now hefting a basket on her hip?

It is my nanny Lammi, in Jakarta, walking in bare feet across the kitchen tiles, her left hip encumbered by the basket she carries, the dark contents dripping, darkening the wicker. She kicks the screen door open and walks into the backyard to spill the basket's greenish-black entrails into the grass. Eels. They writhe and spring as though the ground gave them jolts of electrical shock. Then Lammi goes back into the kitchen and comes out gripping the big knife with the wooden handle wrapped in black tape. It's not without cost I recall her running in the yard, her sarong hiked up past her knees, chasing the eels, chopping all their heads off for soup.

I remember walking with her once near sundown, along the Solo River, where many people had come down to bathe or wash their pots of rice or rinse their clothes. When she had to pee, Lammi walked behind a hedge, where, I knew, wild lemon grass grew among the weeds. I listened, and I heard the trickling sound, and then, a smell rising out of the lemon grass. Sandalwood! I remember my father's sermon on the seed!

He gave it to a handful of people. It was during one of those sunrise services he used to hold at Crooked Creek Forest in Pennsylvania. Usually fifteen or twenty people showed up while the birds were just beginning to pipe, and we all carried tables, food, and pots of coffee up a wooded hill. Then, while we all breakfasted, my father talked, but casually, happy to be out of the pulpit. It was on one of those mornings I first heard of the garden of nutmeg. There abides a living lamp. East of you or me, he claimed, east of even the last man from China, lived a sentient perfume, an inbreathing and uttering seed, our original agent. A volatile plenum, it is an immeasurable plenty; immemorial, it is a pregnant myrrh; the myrrh of myrrhs, it is the mother of spices; the song of songs, it is a fragrant lamp and wholly accomplished, yet perpetually changing score; both the late wine and our original milk, it is a fecund nard. And there go forth from this vital seed figures distilled a day, or a year, or a century; a leaf, a tree, a woman or man, tremulous assays on substantiality, insubstantial. All worlds distilled worlds, all states translations of that first redolence, the very idea of substance is but a poor version of that true irreducible honey. An ark, all fragrance, is our trove, the Seed, stringent past jasmine. "We are embalmed in a shabby human closet," he said. "Get out! Get to the garden of nutmeg." There lay change. Or else we die. And in that wild ultimatum lay our whole inheritance. But I have it all wrong. That was his Thanksgiving message, told in November.

But I remember now it wasn't my father I walked with up a hill, but you. It was night. We'd been traveling a long time to get to that hill, where we climbed up with many strangers, while many more strangers were coming down. And lining the ridge of the hill were many more. And I heard, as we climbed, many languages being spoken, Spanish, English, two or three dialects of Chinese, Russian, Polish. It was too dark to see anyone's face. I could smell food being cooked, and heard babies crying, children laughing. And when it was time, you told me to take off my shoes. So I did, and we climbed the rest of the way barefoot. And when it was time, you spread a blanket, and we sat down. Something was about to happen; everyone was looking in the same direction. And I could see from where we sat that there were other hills with other people standing on them. It was the night of the shooting stars! I remember! It was Chicago. The blanket belonged to your twin sister, Denise. Our niece was there. I called her my little olive. And our sons. They were there, and while I lay there, staring up into a closet of stars, waiting for the streaks, traces of a far broom sweeping, you twin mothers and our children began to sing and tell by turns a story in the round, a story about a needle rowing all night, rowing over and under miles of garment. And when it arrived at the sea, it went on rowing and, arriving at the moon, found it to be no stone of boundary. It was a right-handed needle you sang about, singing thistle, linen, and gorse, sewing the fine and the coarse, sewing a garment for the seed. But what is a needle worth? A needle is only worth its one eye a seed may pass through, a seed that had no place to rest, a seed which, born flying, flew. Awake, my love, don't sleep. It's your birthday. And a seed is on its way, a winged seed. It travels all night to bring you the news: morning glory.

A seed, born flying, flew, knowing nothing else, it flew, and in that persistence resembling praise it took no respite. But its natural course was inevitably radial, away from its birth and into the second day, no frontier, and the seed flew through. And after years of flying over that uninhabitable space—hardly the width of a breath—it eventually exited. Only to begin its longest journey to find its birthplace, that place of eternal unrest. From unrest to unrest it was moving. And without so much as a map to guide it, and without so much as a light. The seed's only companion was the call it heard at its ear, coming from its birthplace, realm of its first day, a call coming from behind it, prior, as it were, to the seed itself. Because of this, the call began to take on all the properties of an urge. And, after all, simultaneous with any true call is the urge to be flying. If only it could turn around, but it couldn't. If only it could fly backward, but it couldn't. Even while its flying was closing the desolate expanses ahead, its flying revealed ever greater expanses behind it. Even as it departed, the seed was already arriving. Only by such loss could the seed possibly own a destiny: the sun.

What was it my father said about the sun? I remember only the sun, a syllable. The nighthawk! There he is again.

Somewhere between his cry, his flight, and his groan, the bird is. And every night it's just me and him. And one of us always goes to sleep before the other. I hope it's me tonight. To stay up past the nighthawk can get lonely. Soon, you're left with not even the sound, but only the thread it sewed through your hair, and someone tapping at a far sill in your brain, asking you to consider the birds. So you do. And find all flying a complex jeopardy, determining the safety of the seed in winter, and the fate of every flower, the outcome of the fruit as well as the ninth house of the sun, and therefore the sun. All flying enacts the sun, our ground, black when you look straight into it, and a pyramid. All flying makes a figure without compass, shapely. All flying. The swallow's and the winged seed's, the dreamer's as well as the hair of the one dreamt, who waits for me, where the morning glory closes at evening. All flying enacts our human evening, except when it enthralls the windows of our morning. All flying is born. Thought is dead. Feeling is black, and there is only feeling, which is flying. And only praise supports it, those two pigeons I caught in the park and pressed to my chest as a boy, their hearts inches from my own unaccountable song. And though those two were not, as I believed, my peak of summer, but lintel and threshold to that vast house their relinquishing made of my heart, vacant and collecting now to itself all flight denied four wings pinned by two hands, while my dumb hunger multiplies its beaks and claws, I've seen such least ones even a boy's heart defeats, gawky walkers at our feet in the cities, I've seen them pitch off high cornices and fall as though struck, only to open

the winged seed

at the impossible moment and, rising, defy.

Defy. For by defiance do I name my earth upright, my ground this startled home, my bell longing for the hand that sows, by hard rows at a standing rope, the boundaries of this hour, whose circumference, whispered to a folded wing for safekeeping, is told to alter the air for miles inside the country where a woman waits for me. She is dressing for our journey together, combing her hair opposite the direction of this, my approach, continuous with summer, graduating past winter, synchronous twice, rhyming with death and time.

Night brims the rose and exceeds it, requires its passing into an inextinguishable noon, surpasses the aspiring steeple as well as this moment in which the rose overstays the reaches of the voice of the bell. Night supports the seeds, on which every table stands, on which is spread a feast, and the one missing for hundreds of years comes, trampling the dew on the overgrown brick path. His countenance poses a question to our fervor, we who manage night only by an equal ardor, that singular bird maintained at a fountainhead, whose stemming is an almost human throat.

Only night which graduates to cloth, whose measure exceeds the width of a bolt and the length of the farthest arm, and woven at the rate of birds and wild grasses, as well as the more general passage of the sea, whose greater waves contain the smaller, to carry string and other things we lost, thistle, linen, and gorse . . . what did he say about the night? Does it matter, now that he's dead? What did he say about death? Something to do with ladders, a cleft broom, black seeds and white seeds. What seeds? Shall we look inside the hourglass my father kept in his pocket? Through that waist salt crowds to fall into heaps, unresolved; Tuesday, Wednesday, thistle, linen, and gorse.

Give me night itself, a waist of silk and immediate port, a myriad corner continuing; in your wrist and foot such arrival, and you are so near; lid and dark lash, you are such ankle; I can hardly say what elbow there is in the course of your river; nor what dark birds fly opposite our sleeping together, what winter oncoming. Therefore I keep my hand moving over you, all the while knowing my hand may not move from glory to glory without it first moving shore to shore, your rib to hipbone, where, paused, my hand thinks with its wrist, the blood keeping count, as when the chariot, carrying two riders, flies down the stairs, the career of the vehicle gone to what's singing, loose in the driver's elbows, while the archer, braided, is let entirely to riding a swiveled bearing and axle tree, and the age beginning with the Yellow Emperor continues through me, whose history is in my face, my undoubled lid and alien eye, whose future is a question forming between my thighs, while you keep, or spend, which is a further range of keeping, the answer to our sufficiency, bed for seed.

Moving, my hand traverses you infinitely. Yet, once only, and once again, your width little less than an arm thrown across the recorder bird's dark note, going, gone.

Therefore, tell me, my love, by what motion of my hands may I gather you, by what action of the soul might I compass, having no hope to encompass, by what gladness of heart earn, your fragrant company? You I turn to one night, not halfway through our journey together, and ask, *What, Woman, will you give me for all these white petals?*

And you answer, *My one clasp you may unclasp. And this green basket.*

But *What, Woman, for this stone in my shoe?* I wanted to know.

You said, *The name of the stone, which is Death, and these peaches, one ripening a minute later than the first.*

And when I ask my mother, *Mother, what will you give me for this silver mirror?* she says, *All mirrors tell the same lie. What else have you to trade?* I answer, *This fish head. Good,* she answers, *I'll give it back to you the way you like it, with ginger, miso, green onion, the eyes steamed to succulent jelly. Plus the rich brain,* she says, *You may eat the rich brain.* I thank her. *For you,* I say, *I will fry the tail.*

IT'S CLEAR I got my appetite from my father, my taste for brains and eyes. And though no one taught him to play he pulled on his accordion and closed it, opened and folded it, rocking and leaning, while his left foot counted, and his right-hand fingers jumped up and down the ladder of black and bone-colored keys to his old Harmonymaker Club Modell, German-made, which he bought in China, when he was twenty-one, before I ever came, sat down beside him, and listened. He's been

dead eleven years. I'm the age he was when I was born in
Indonesia. In Pennsylvania, in a kitchen no one may enter again, ever, he played while my mother sang, her
voice kept a little ahead of the vertical ribs of the fanning and collapsing organ.

But do I make too much of something only one of
three remembers, when that one himself will someday
be forgotten? What abides? Is it day or night forming
ahead of us? Already I feel I've been here a long time.

I've been sitting up at this window so many successive
nights in a row, the wrens and pigeons on the sill fear me
less. Though I may never touch them. Yet, we'll minister
to each other come morning, my China, their Japan. I
think it's of seeds they trill and scrape, and rich garbage
in the alleys of Chicago, where any evening or morning
you might find me three stories up from Lawrence Av-
enue, and not half an hour from last night's dream, in
which what was omitted included the dreamer, who
went on orbiting the sun with the rest of the house of
sleepers, their animals, birds in the rafters, brooms, and
other insomniacs.

It has been late a long time, and getting later as I go
on outliving those voices in a singing manse-kitchen in
Pennsylvania, whose door opened onto seven steps
down to a path that led, turning once to the right—
enough time to touch the ivy—to lead four stairs up to
the black-banded, red double doors, the right one of
which swung toward you to let into the vestibule, in
whose cool dark you could stand a moment and listen to
the creaking and ticking in the nave, where no one

came on weekdays but me, for nothing except to sit and count two heavens: one in the manse-kitchen and one in the empty rows of pews, while a third, or a fourth or four-thousandth is even now getting made beyond any hearing we might intend on earth.

Heaven is let. There are no keys. The side door to my father's church was never locked, yet when I went back a year ago, two years, three, the doors were dead-bolted. I knocked. I knocked again. I went away. Anyway, what was I doing there? In heaven, my father sneezes and turns right to left the page of the book that's read back and forth, no book the living read except we write it day and night, now as in childhood.

Now and in childhood, it is the same solitude, immense, me waiting for my sister. And when she comes, I'll hand her all my roses, and she'll turn over to me her best hours, her two living streams, *And all my wine*, she adds. Yes, all her good wine, and not one moment too soon, not one promise promised not simultaneously fulfilled, not one vow spoken not the same time kept.

When my little brother stood as high as my shoulder, I took his hand and stood half a head shorter than our older brother, who in turn stood up to our sister's shoulder, past which her straight black hair fell all the way to her hip. And though we held hands and followed our parents through street after street of cold air and our first winter in America, stared at by passersby for reasons not clear to us, though we walked linked like that, we knew there were two of us missing: a brother in China our parents hadn't heard from in years, and a brother buried in

Indonesia, neither of whom our parents talked about in front of us, except sometimes to mention a certain Cemetery of the Red Plaque, a detail in their conversations like the only piece left of a greater puzzle. In fact, it was the Chinese graveyard in Jakarta where our brother was buried, and which, years later, I visited with my sister, but only to discover he was now lying under seven strangers, the permanent residents there heaped atop each other over the years. The blackened gravestones, like giant molars, were crowded and unkempt, while among them roved groups of beggars who followed us from stone to stone. They surrounded us, empty hands extended, even while we stood in dumb silence at the broken marker our parents had so many years ago planted. Only as we were leaving did we notice the faded red plaque hanging on the front gate's square post. Effaced of any word, it bore only a faint gold letter R.

Our first Christmas Eve in America, our parents took us to the Sears & Roebuck in East Liberty where we were each given a quarter to spend at the gum ball and novelty vending machines that stood arrayed at the department store's entrance. We had little money; my father, at the age of forty, was starting a new life as a student at the Pittsburgh Theological Seminary; my mother had already pawned a jade carving of a hare to see us through the months of November and December. At home, a leafless branch my father broke off a tree served as our *Tannenbaum*, which he and my mother decorated with white paper birds they made, no two alike, and each bearing inside it a birthday candle.

It was my sister's idea that the children should exchange gifts by allowing each to ask of his siblings one thing each desired from among the other's belongings. So it was, she laid out her keepsakes on the kitchen table, from which I chose two walnuts, reddish-brown from her constant fondling in her coat pocket, and my brothers each chose a fountain pen and a comic book. Then each of us laid out our own treasures, and I gave up a new pencil, a lock without a key, and a magnet. At midnight, our mother brought out a bowl of oranges, and we all sat in our parents' bedroom telling stories and eating the fruit our mother peeled with such skill we tasted no skin or rind.

I remember the dark wood bureau that sat in the corner of my father's study. Inside each of its fifty little drawers, and wrapped in brown oil paper or tucked in a musty envelope, was some gnarled root or petrified mushroom, a dried shard of shark fin or ground-up deer horn. There were dried skeletons of sea horses and lumps of desiccated bear gall. There was all manner of parts of finned and winged things my father would chop or shave or mince, then measure with a tiny, long-handled, silver teaspoon, and mix in a bowl of hot water to be drained when any one of us was suffering from forgetfulness or bad dreams. I remember a polished scale and its meticulous needle that sat under a red velvet coverlet, and the sets of silver acupuncture needles of varying lengths and finenesses, and the figurine of a reclining woman, whose nude ivory surface was covered with tiny black characters, etched at each nerve center and nexus.

I remember the bitter odors the drawers yielded upon my opening them. I smelled it on my father's neck when he bent down and kissed me, who lay in my childhood fevers, dreaming of rope, thick, hairy braids, and mouse whiskers, twitch, twitch-twitch.

I recall a wood-plank bridge strung high over a chasm in Indonesia, a green gorge sheer to black depths, from which there rose, whole, a single huge blooming mist. And we crossed over, deaf in the roar of the mother of waters below, our eyes turned inward, negotiating that awe-ful vastness at a self-gathering gaze, even while our eyes stayed open to it all. We crossed in single file, a sister, a brother, and the woman Lammi, carrying me.

As we inched along the narrow transition, a bridge designed, perhaps, by a native man with a spidery brain, there issued from Lammi's mouth radiant arrows, spells to preserve our crossing over. After crossing, we climbed a skinny path through many leaves and colors of leaves, trees and submarine shades, all the patterns repeated in Lammi's skirt, a batik wrap. And I remember broken panels of sunlight, like magnificent ruined stairs.

I am in a cloth sling, riding Lammi's hip. I see Lammi. I know her by her smell, ripe fruit and seaweed. I am in the jungle, on the narrow but well-worn path made by feet before our own. We're on the island of Java and crossing a ravine to the other side and a group of houses, and one in particular, where the people slept in one room and goats and pigs slept in another. In the daytime, they live together, people and animals. Night brings a feeling of alarm, the sense that soon I might see

t
h
e

w
i
n
g
e
d

s
e
e
d

something I should not. So I pay especially close attention, waiting for the thing I shouldn't see, so I can close my eyes in time. When I think of that house where the people and animals live, the adults seem in a panic now, locking doors and bolting window shutters, herding the animals into their den of hay. Night. A baby is crying. One of the goats has given birth, and the smell of the wet newborn and the afterbirth has brought a tiger out of the jungle. The whole village is anxious. The men wear long knives and sit awake all night with their antique guns.

Some days we walked through a dry clay field beyond the village limits, and I was always amazed that Lammi could walk for miles with a thorn deep in her heel, the soles of her feet were so toughened. Some days a naked boy followed us for a while, one of the neighbor's children. He cavorted and scowled and, turning his hands into claws, howled and made gestures as though he would attack us, while Lammi kept shooing him away like any wild dog. Frothing at the mouth, showing us the whites of his eyes, sometimes he tried to urinate on us as we walked, or, running a few yards ahead of us, he squatted, his genitals staring at us, and waited for us to go by, on our way past the railroad tracks, and past the last whitewashed cement-walled houses on the outskirts of the city.

Only three years old, and Lammi's favorite, I rode on her hip during most of the hour-long walk, both of us sweating, her maroon, fruit-skin-dyed sarong darkening in stripes down her back, her ribs, between her breasts.

Fei and Go ran ahead at first, hiding from each other, then crashing through the foliage screaming, sending lizards darting and birds squawking and scattering. But soon they tired, and straggled behind Lammi. They clung to her sarong, and we walked a ways like that, Lammi's strong, young woman's body dragging two little ones and carrying a third into the island's dense, humid jungle.

And if the coffin maker walked by, cheap coffins piled monumentally on his horizontal back, we all fell silent, knowing better than to say anything to him. Once, Fei pointed and said, *Look!* at which the carrier of those wooden rectangular boxes, without stopping, looked back at us under his burden, and laughed, toothless, *They're for your mummy and daddy, missy. Better get home before I do.*

The air was a hot body pressing on us. There was about it a languorous intent, moist against our necks, between our legs, between Lammi's body and mine. My head lolled, I closed my eyes. I could hear their feet treading, and Lammi's short breaths. I could hear her sarong, tight around her legs, plucked like a drum as she walked. Around her waist, my thighs grew wet.

After a while, she peeled me off her body and made me walk a little of the way. But I wanted to ride, and tugged at her hand until she stopped, squatted down with her back to me, and I straddled her hips again. With her brown arms strung behind her, her fingers locked into a seat under me, we went on.

"Will the tiger," Fei pants, "will the tiger still be

there?" Lammi explains that the tiger was part of a traveling circus that's probably in another village on the other side of the city by now.

Soon we will arrive at her village and be given water, something to eat, slices of jackfruit, or the translucent, sweet jellylike meat of green coconuts. Then Lammi will disappear somewhere, and we'll be taken with the village children to watch the puppet show.

Lammi is nineteen, a child really, her body dense, yet compact. And though Fei and Go and I don't know it, each time after she leaves us with her family, she goes to meet her lover. But one day we will find this out, happening upon them by accident. Then it will be up to Fei, oldest of the three of us, to explain what goes on.

But though Lammi is just a girl, to me she already smells like one of the grown-ups; she is already suffused with that scent, powerful and ancient. Mu smells of it as well; on Lammi, it is coconut oil, dust, sweat, and hair. It is the smell of sex and decay.

And I remember now how Su betrayed us. And there wasn't a thing we could do about it. It was her body that betrayed us and we should have known it would happen, but we didn't know, how could we?

Su was Seeti and Lammi's youngest sister. She came to us a little older than Fei. Her coming among us in the middle of the night was announced by the sound of women's voices quarreling and a girl's intermittent weeping. My mother followed the sounds to where the servants lived in a small house behind ours and found Su squatting on the floor and Lammi and Seeti arguing

above her head. The older sisters explained that their
brother had brought Su from their village and left her
with them. He insisted he could no longer support her
since he was taking a third wife who was pregnant with
his child. He left Lammi and Seeti to argue over what to
do with Su. Mu said that if the girl liked, she could stay
with us and Mu would ask around about jobs. She was
only two years older than Fei, and soon became as one of
the children. Until her body betrayed us.

The bright anklets of sudden blood were the beginning. She wiped them away with a corner of her sarong
and as she did we could see how they were attached to
slim rivulets, delicate chains of blood running up the in-
sides of her calves and past her thighs. And all the rich-
est, most frightening hue of red-going-black. When she
wiped, she tended to smear the blood over her legs, leaving a pink cast to them. And now Su was leaving drops
and patches of blood on the kitchen tile, on the teak
floors, and wiping up after herself, while her older sisters
scolded her, and Mu firmly asked her not to go around
naked under her sarong.

All of it was inconsequential to us, the children.
What mattered was that she was no longer one of us.
She was bloody. She was a shocking body, a mysterious
and frightening planet. She possessed a sex.

Of course, we always knew Su was a *girl*, just as we
knew Fei was a *girl*, and Go, Tai, and I were *boys*. But I
don't think we understood that our genders were con-
nected intimately with our sex. I remember our being
curious about one another's bodies, but I think we

sensed a lightness to ourselves where we perceived an almost nauseating gravity to adults. We were transparent. After all, we existed only when someone saw us. And mostly no one saw us. For the most part we lived unrecognized, unacknowledged except in the most basic ways: food was set out for us, clothes were set out for us, we were told to do and to not do. All of it while the adults went about their serious business. Our world was beside the point.

But Su's betrayal was undeniable. She would soon consider suitors and spend less time with us. She would soon become like her sisters, who walked down the streets in a hail of whistles and tongues clicking. And that iron odor, it was hopeless.

My sister recalls how night after night, after our mother came back among us, after the servants offered to cook her dinner and she refused it, Mu walked through the tall doorway of her dark room and closed one of the narrow double doors, half her room illuminated by an angular light falling from the hall, and the other half, where she lay, dark. Night after night she lay the same, in her slip, in the dark, on half of the bed, and chewed her lip, one naked arm straight by her side, the other thrown across her eyes, not sleeping, but going. While we lay down with her on our father's side of the bed and one by one we fell asleep to the sound of our sister whispering consolations to our mother, Mu glowed in her slip. To where was our Mu going? We hadn't the least idea, but we knew none of us could follow. Each day she was more gone, less and less with us. The signs were the hairs on her pillow each morning, her body going narrow, her skin frighteningly white.

In May of 1961, our father had already been in prison for a year, charged with working for the CIA in plans to bomb military installations on the island of Java, and spreading discontent by preaching ideas from the West. But while blueprints taken from his office only showed plans for classroom buildings, copies of certain letters proved incriminating enough for Sukarno to have him taken from his home by armed men. The squad of booted and uniformed men marching up our steps and the sight of four big army jeeps idling in our narrow street, which was barely wide enough for the coffee seller and the coconut peddler to pass shoulder to shoulder trundling their pushcarts, was enough of a signal to the entire neighborhood that we'd become pariahs. Anyone associating with us risked the same treatment. From that day on, even friends stopped coming by.

He was, of course, innocent from the start. My father was one of the most nonpolitical persons I've ever known. If there was ever a man who abhorred all politics, despised all parties, believed almost mystically that all actions of government, no matter how well-intended, created evil, it was my father. But suspicion fell on him because, first of all, he was Chinese, and then because, as vice president of Gamaliel University, he'd invited a number of teachers and scholars from seminaries all over the United States to visit Jakarta as part of an exchange program, and he had on one occasion housed a minister from Ohio. Such associations while Sukarno was trying to ally himself with China and Russia could not be tolerated. When two men from the Indonesian War Administration confronted my father with what they referred to as the insurrectionary and seditious nature of the courses offered at the newly opened university, and suggested he change the curriculum and get rid of the foreign professors, he thanked them for their advice and said politely, though emphatically, he could not. So they put him away and closed the university. Every day of that time, and for twelve or fourteen hours a day, our mother spent shifting her weight from one leg to the other as she stood at the prison gate, or in one of the queues outside one or another office of the administration.

If she were at the prison gate, it meant she'd given up on the bureaucracy of the War Administration, and had decided to take the chance that she might see Ba beyond the fences, walking in the exercise yard, and then she'd know he wasn't dead. Or else she might see him being herded with others onto a truck headed for she didn't know where, and no one would tell her. Her standing there could also mean she'd actually secured a visitor's permit from the administration, and was now showing it to one of the guards at the gate. On that day, it was up to the guard if she got to see Ba, and always he said *Wait now.* And then he returned to chatting with the other uniformed men, or napping in the guardhouse, or turning the pages of a magazine, or strolling the width of the gate, or else just sitting and smoking the cigarettes Mu had given him. And then another man would come

forward to ask what she wanted. Sometimes he would
ask in a genuinely kind tone and, just as kindly, he too
would say *Wait now.* One after another the men asked to
see Mu's paper, and one after another they nodded
knowingly as they perused it, then handed it back to her.
Sometimes, one of them would look at it and put it back
in her hand without saying a word. But Mu knew what
his stern silence meant: *Wait now.* There was always a
group of women like Mu at the gate, and at some point,
usually after the day had long grown old, one of the men
would suddenly point to one of the women and open the
gate for her. It wasn't ever clear why any particular one
of them was granted entrance, and then the others
would walk shyly with paper in hand toward the iron
opening, wide enough for one to pass, and the man
would hold up a white-gloved hand and say the two
words which could mean, depending on the tone and
inflection, a richly varied number of things. *Dear ladies,
you must wait now,* or *Silly hens, I'm enjoying a cigarette
now,* or *Did you think a few rupiahs and chocolate bars
were enough to soften me?* or *Now, rich little white faces,
certainly you can afford more than this?* or *I am a busy man
of the state, I can hardly be bothered with your pieces of paper and whining now.* The same two words repeated over
and over, each man saying them with his own voice, his
own brand of feeling, weighing the words differently
from his fellow man, each mouth, each breath uttering
toward the women, *Wait now.*

Sometimes Mu got in to see Ba. Many times she stood
through two guard shifts and went home with the useless

permit in her purse, knowing she would have to return to the administration the next morning and apply for a new one. The administration was housed in a large, two-story, white-columned building left over from the time of the colonists. Inside, hundreds of people, mostly women, could be found waiting in the drab, badly lit, high-ceilinged offices and hallways. Some of them carried suitcases filled with papers and documents, ready to enter an elaborate maze of departments and divisions and branches of divisions. And each officer passed her applications for Ba's release to the next, and every shunting of her file and question from her mouth was necessarily attended by money or cigarettes. For every doorway could be traversed only by bribery, and the walls were adorned with calendars of pretty girls or posters of Sukarno.

At best, her requests were treated like news from home. Under these circumstances, the man or men chatted with her like old acquaintances, taking her money even as they nodded in sympathy or shook their heads in amazement at the effort she'd expended to get even this far. At worst, they squinted behind cigarette smoke, took her money, and told her her situation was hopeless, and that Ba was most likely dead. It was an obstacle course whose corridors and rooms near the entrance were jammed with anyone who could afford the trifling price of a compliment or a pack of cigarettes, while the halls and offices on the second floor grew less crowded as only the most resourceful could go on, those who could afford to traffic in radios, phonographs, or more expensive favors. And everyone who entered had the same objectives: to find out where someone had disappeared to, to finagle a permit, or, for the most determined, to negotiate someone's release from Glodok Prison or Tjipinang, or, worst of all, Unrest Island.

Each morning before she left, while the servants Seeti, Lammi, and Ebu sat on the floor around her, Mu sat on the edge of her bed and combed her waist-length hair as she divided the day's duties among them and decided the day's menu. Then she handed them the money they would require for that day's purchases, and she always gave them more than they would need, knowing they would pocket the extra for a sick relative or a newborn in their own household. It was a tacit agreement between her and them, and mutually beneficial. After she dismissed them, she called in the children. Every day since the day Ba had been taken from us, Mu had rehearsed with us the procedures we would need to take in case a fire broke out on our street, an almost daily occurrence that time of year in Jakarta, a city where grass huts stood alongside other homes.

She stroked her daughter's arms gently, and asked, *Do you remember?* And Fei recited the procedures out loud to her, after which our mother commanded, *Go ahead,* at which time Fei knelt down, maneuvering her leg brace in both hands with the ease of the long acquainted, and undid the false bottom panel of the nightstand. Then she reached inside and pulled out a flat metal strongbox. Then quickly she lifted off of her neck the string hung there, and from its ring of keys she found the one marked by red nail polish which would undo the lock.

At nine years old, Fei was put in charge of the house while Mu was gone, and she wore around her neck all of the keys to her mother's locks. After undoing the strongbox and putting the string back around her neck, Fei opened the lid to the box and took out the leather satchel that contained all of Mu's gems and neat stacks of money bound in rubber bands. Ducking under the satchel's thick strap, she hung it across her slight chest and shoulder, and then took me and my brother, ages three and five, by the hand, and turned to stand inspection before our mother, knowing full well the weight of what she carried: namely, everything Mu and Ba were worth in paper and hardest stone, and everything worth saving, should fire take the house. Mu looked at us a while.

Many years later, my mother would tell me that although she had always been pleased, even proud, of Fei as we practiced the fire drill, she always experienced, like a knotted rope in the middle of her chest, an inexplicable pain at the sight of the little girl running through the steps with such unquestioning efficiency. There were times, she tried to explain, when as she watched Fei she suddenly had the feeling that she wasn't looking at a girl at all. And at those moments she wasn't sure what she was looking at, some strange creature for whom childhood was erased, even as she continued to inhabit a child's body. And all the while the little creature didn't know to ask for a childhood, didn't know, wouldn't know until late, much too late, that she was giving up being a child even as she remained one in so many ways.

And when our mother asked, *And now? And now*, Fei would begin reciting, finishing the drill, *I call Lammi, Seeti, and Ebu into the front yard, lock all of the doors, then go and watch.* Fei knew that behind the locked gate of the front courtyard of our Dutch-built house, we could stand safe to watch if a fire from a nearby hut or one of the other houses might spread to our home, in which instance, and only then, Fei was to unlock the front gates and lead us all to safety. But if the flames were being successfully contained by rescuers, we were to remain behind the gate, in order not to risk being robbed on the street or having our house ransacked. But because a conflagration could spread among the grass huts and timber houses unpredictably and with terrifying speed, engulfing whole homes in seconds, the decision of how long we remained behind the gates before we exposed ourselves to danger in the streets and our house to looting would rest entirely on the wisdom of Fei's judgment. Mu explained this to Fei again and again, making certain she understood the importance of her complete and unflinching attention in that circumstance, and the gravity of her role in general under the extreme conditions in which we had recently found ourselves.

Fei bore it undaunted, and with little effect but for a growing sadness which went unnoticed at the time, perhaps even by herself, so naturally a part of her it had become, and ineffable. Mu recalls that Fei hardly ever cried. Except during her long stays in the hospital after repeated surgery on her hip, when she would beg to be taken home. Photos of her at that age consistently reveal a girl withstanding. Whether modeling a new dress, or pushing Tai in a baby carriage, or showing off a paper umbrella, whether in a steep shadow, or in the glaring light of a Jakarta afternoon, she appears in each case in the ubiquitous leg brace, a contraption twice the size of her leg, and she stares straight out with an expression which is a mixture of fear, determination, and an unaccountable look of knowing, steeling herself against whatever approaches from beyond the borders of the photograph.

I remember waiting for Fei as she crossed the Solo on a ferry. Precariously over water she is coming and I am drawing her to the shore. She is balanced, coming over water, between the shore from which she stepped onto the skiff and the shore on which I stand, between her deep reflection which slides along beneath her and which is seen only by me, between that watery self and the air, between herself and nothing, she is coming, perched lightly at the back of a skiff carrying two other passengers and the boat's pilot, a skinny little man whose face is cleaved from his neck by the shadow of his straw hat. Fei is leaning against her red bicycle, her hand on the handlebars, as the little man with brown arms and no face pilots his boat toward me. When she reaches the shore, the pilot will lift the bicycle to set it on land, and I'll get on the back of it, and Fei will pedal like mad up the dirt path.

Years later I will be gliding over water at evening. The boat I will be on then will be between two countries. The captain of that boat will point into darkness and say, *If it were day you would be able to see Indonesia very clearly at the horizon. It's too bad, a shame, since by daylight we'll be miles from seeing it.* Darkness, first, then distance, would prevent me from seeing the body of the country in which I was born and where I stood once on a riverbank waiting for Fei to come.

It was her face Mu saw first behind the bars of the front gate one night when she came home to find the entire length of our block pulsing in the wild glow and immense shadows of burning houses. The street was too crowded for the pedicab and Mu had to get out at one end of it and run to the other end, making her way through a mob of gawkers, looters, and neighbors. Whole families of women and children cried out, helpless as they watched demonic figures jumping into the flames that consumed their houses and running back out carrying furniture, pots and pans, clothing. The men of the households haggled desperately with a serenely disinterested fire department chief over a reasonable price for the service of turning on the hoses. There behind the gate of her own home, Mu's daughter stood, laden with satchel, at the head of brothers and a houseful of servants, oblivious to Mu coming toward her, staring and studying the progress of the inferno four doors down, her body almost pressed to the gate, a scarf of shadow flying about her face, her black eyes illuminated by the burning.

The water hoses got turned on that night, but not before six homes were burned to the ground, along with a Chinese herb shop, whose owner had ended up handing over almost all of his briefcase of money to the firemen, only to lose his business completely. It was for just such a catastrophe that Mu prepared us, rehearsing with us the fire drill each morning.

Then she would leave with a lunch tin containing our father's favorite foods which Ebu had prepared, and almost every night she returned, the food cold and untouched in its containers.

Mu was getting devoured. First, there was Ba's absence, which ate her daily, leaving her thin; her eyes stared and looked bruised, Fei recalls. And the other men ate her, the ones at every Administration doorway, the ones at the prison gate. Not only was her body becoming lighter, so was her purse, and eventually her house. One day a group of soldiers arrived in a truck to seize our belongings. They confiscated not only all of the papers which pertained to our father's work at the university, but his desk as well, and two sofas that sat in his study. And then more men came, the ones dressed in shabby uniforms and sandals, wild, hungry-looking men who materialized all over the city, who capitalized on the chaos that was spreading all over the city.

A few times a week a group of two or three such men would arrive at our gate and demand to be let in. Mu stood a few feet from the bars and spoke to them. She fluctuated between harsh suspicion and respectful courtesy depending on what she perceived was the most useful tone. Sometimes the men would wave a stack of

papers covered in official seals and claim to have orders
to remove our furniture. Mu could usually get rid of
them by asking to see their papers and telling them to
meet her the next day at the War Administration offices, where she could get someone to translate the documents for her. Having hoped for easier prey, these men
would usually take their papers and go. The bolder ones
were more dangerous. They made outright threats such
as, *I know where the master of the house is locked away. Just
let my friends and me have a look around.* They meant that
if we didn't give them something, anything, they could
get to Ba. There was no knowing if they were telling the
truth and no point in doubting them. So Mu would have
to hand them a few dollars through the gate's black bars.
Still other nights, if we knew they were coming, we
turned out the lights and sat quietly in Mu's room,
where we lay perfectly still.

And then the downfall of ice began.

The first evening of the icefall, Mu was home, everyone was indoors, and nobody understood what was happening to us. We all sat on our mother's bed in dumb
fear as our roof roared under showering ice until we
thought the ceiling would cave in. When the noise
stopped, we found the yard and the flat roof of our house
paved with hailstones the size of golf balls. Apparently,
ours was the only house on the block that had been
bombarded. Standing at the front gate was a throng of
neighbors and passersby staring at our home and asking
what had happened; some of them reaching
through the bars and scooping handfuls of ice, laughing

in amazement at the cold pearls melting on their hands in the leaden heat of evening. The second night it happened, a week later, Mu was not at home, and we sat while Seeti, Lammi, and Ebu rocked and chanted prayers and spells against demons, and the ice pounded our house.

The police suspected vandals, but could not explain how anyone could get that much ice in Jakarta. When it persisted, they advised us, as the servants had been doing all along, to consult a mystic, or offer sacrifices to the gods. So it was, we found ourselves one day, standing in the shade of a banyan tree, while Lammi repeated the broken phrases of a prayer. I remember how unlikely the shrine seemed with its foot-high elephant god standing inside a closet not much bigger. Disappointed by its size, by its resemblance to the cheap curios we'd seen for sale in the stalls of the open-air market, and tired from our morning-long journey to find the idol, my sister, my brothers, and I, dwarfed by the huge banyan trees overhead, watched as Lammi performed her ritual, the ground around her littered with flowers, fresh and days dead, the offerings of other believers.

We'd made the trip here following the advice of a local wizard, for not only were the ice showers continuing, but our home had recently been, according to the servants, visited by a spirit who would not leave. They called it "the ethereal one," or, "the one who mourns for a body to inhabit," or, "the one who went out flying one day and lost his way and ended up trapped in a house," and they claimed that it was continually crying, sometimes so loud and baleful it kept them awake at night. Of course, we could not hear it. Though as soon as I said that, I heard it. As soon as I thought to say that Fei, Go, Tai, and I could not hear it, I immediately heard what I did not, could not, hear way back then, when I was a child on Java, what the servants claimed to have heard, a sound coming from some place in the house: the sobbing of a child, a spectral, lonely sound, inconsolable.

The servants had been hearing it ever since we moved into the new house, and though they mentioned it only infrequently to Ba or Mu, their talk in front of us was full of dark admonishments and supernatural entanglements. We were warned of the possibility that a malevolent spirit might make itself visible to us in the form of a huge, black-skinned baby baring pointed teeth, in which instance our only hope was to gather our courage, face it, and shout *Amen!* which would frighten the demon away. It seemed a simple enough trick, except Sheeti told us that the demon was aware of this charm, and would sneak up on its victim and frighten him, then grab the victim's dumbstruck tongue in its claw, and try to tear it out of his mouth. Ebu told us about a case of possession she had witnessed as a child.

The complete nature of the spirit in our house remained uncertain to even Lammi, Seeti, and Ebu. Lammi was sure it was a child. Ebu said probably an Arab. Seeti was convinced it was male, and that it had come from Jerusalem on the wind. And while no two were in complete agreement as to what its intentions were, no two of them had even remotely the same idea as to where a heaven like a Real Jerusalem might be, Sheeti beautifully certain it was the capital of Rome, and Ebu crustily claiming that her great-great-grandfather, on a military expedition with the Second Prince of the Royal Court, had passed through a magnificent city by that name which was located north of the Great Wall of China. A shrunken, toothless woman of about fifty, whose skin was mottled as old vellum betraying repeated erasures, Ebu told us about an uninhabitable and immeasurable expanse of wind-scoured, rocky plain, where a city suddenly, defiantly jutted up its ramparts and towers. It was called Jerusalem, and it was, at the time of the Second Prince's visit, a great seat of learning, trade, military power, sorcery, and magic, ruled by an Arab people who were as brutal as they were faithful to the very gods Lammi, Sheeti, and Ebu worshiped. Who were their gods? While the gods of the West were primarily bearded men, the East's deities were animals and naked dancing women and children. What were their names? The three women weren't always in accord on that issue, but they were sure that one of the ethereal ones was among us, and that he had to be fed. Its diet, however, was a point of contention. So they took turns, each of them leaving a different food out each day for "the one who recently died and while on his way to the other world got lost and now is trapped between two worlds."

Lammi lay three leaves at the bottom of a bowl, crossed at the stems so they looked like green tail feathers. From the blackened cooking pot just lifted from the

fire, she scooped with her bare fingers a lump of the
noontime rice, and, while blowing to cool it, formed it
quickly into a neat ball, which she placed on top of the
leaves. Only after she placed the bowl in an inconspicu-
ous place, so Mu couldn't readily see it, at the foot of a
mango tree that stood by the front gate of our house, did
all of us eat lunch, squatting in the little yard behind the
house, Fei, Go, and I, using bowls and chopsticks, while
the servants used their fingers, and ate from a common
bowl, deftly gathering the food without letting fall even
a kernel of it, and then tearing a banana leaf and folding
it into a pocket to drink their soup. Tai, our youngest
brother, hardly a year old, was fed by Fei, who chewed
mouthfuls of food and passed it from her mouth to his.
Each day at noon, we ate behind the main house, by the
wooden structure that housed the kitchen next to the
servants' quarters, and a bowl of food was always left at
the front of the house in the same place. Lammi offered
basil and rice, because the ethereal one was a shape-
changer; Seeti, flowers and slices of sweet potato, because those things befitted his caste; Ebu a bowl of
incense and a little cup of rice wine, because he was
Arab.

Though their stories troubled our sleep and shadowed
our waking, we loved to hear them, thick with the
breath that told them. When we asked Mu about the
things we heard told, she reminded us that the servants
were native women, naturally given to sensational story-
telling, idle gossip, and superstition, all three tendencies
harmless if we only avoided taking them seriously. *Only*

stories, were always Mu's final words. Yet, though we might have believed that about Ebu, who inspired slim confidence with her advice that we dab chile paste on Tai's head as a protective charm, and her blind left eyeball in which was embedded, like a tiny embryo in a specimen jar, some indeterminate gray matter, regarding our nannies, we were certain they had access to something wholly forbidden to us, perhaps because we were children, or because we were Chinese. Besides, Seeti and Lammi spoke *our* language, Javanese, the children's language, while Mu, who spoke Chinese to us, spoke the adults' language. Our lives began to grow into a double wakefulness, for even as we went casually about the diurnal activities which adhered to an adult world, something, or else someone, in each of us was continually poised, expectant and ready, in case something beyond that world should suddenly make itself evident. We felt both less substantial and more, for we couldn't tell if we inhabited a world densely populated by three or four orders of beings, as the stories suggested we did, or if we were stranded on an island adrift in some old, measureless sea of anonymous powers which constantly threatened to overcome our finite ground.

I remember sitting with Fei on the ground by the rock and plaster wall that surrounded our home. She was singing to me and mixing mud and flowers in a pot with a spoon when her voice suddenly stopped, her hands fell still. While she stared blankly, I knew immediately she must be listening for the crying, and as I moved out of the sunlight and nearer to her, I listened for it myself,

unable to hear anything but the voices and bicycle bells
in the street beyond the wall. Slowly Fei's hands began
to move again, and her voice began to sing again, but
softer. So it was that the ethereal one's crying, even
while we could not hear it, made itself felt by us, creat-
ing inside our days moments of intense listening, inter-
vals of attention when we tried to hear beyond the din
of every day in Jakarta.

We continually asked to hear the stories. And Mu's
verdict that they *were* stories had little or no effect on
their potency. We *knew* they were stories, which fact
never conflicted with their emotional accuracy. Something in them felt true to us. To be precise, it was the stories behind the stories which felt true to us, those stories
Seeti and Lammi would begin to tell only after the other
stories were told. For inevitably, after all the talking
about so-and-so's brother who was pushed out of a tree
by a spirit, or a respectable merchant who suddenly went
around defecating on people until he was cured, after all
the tales were told which amounted to gossip, Sheeti
and Lammi would begin to tell the larger stories, the stories about the first men and women on Java. It didn't
matter that Java was not really the center of the universe, or that the Javanese weren't, in fact, descendants
of the body parts of a dismembered god. It hardly mattered to us if Sukarno wasn't, in fact, a descendant of the
gods come to call the Javanese back to their rightful
home. We were convinced by the stories behind the stories that our island of cities and rice fields, forests, rivers,
and volcanoes was The World. The greater stories per-

suaded us that our father being jailed, along with so many other fathers of Chinese households, had to do with something much older and darker than what could be explained by adult words like politics or economics. The greater stories called to some correspondent thing inside us that resisted a name, something barely apprehended and timeless.

The stories were true in the same way that the plays which our nannies took us to see were true. We knew that the pieces of wood cut in the shapes of gravestones and lined up in close rows to look like a cemetery were half the size of real gravestones in the real cemetery. And we noticed that the square-shouldered, square-headed dummy bound in a white sheet and carried in on a plank of wood wasn't exactly shaped like the corpses we'd seen carried through the streets during local funeral ceremonies. But when, in the forest, in a low, dim, grass-roofed hut no bigger than our living room, my sister, my brothers, and I watched the performances, we were watching our true hopes and fears clairvoyantly figured.

Sitting on a dirt floor with Seeti and Lammi, in a packed crowd of their village and family members that filled half the circle of the bamboo and wicker enclosure, we were transported as soon as the play began with its usual flourish of cymbals and gongs crashing, pipes blowing. The actors sometimes danced their roles, frequently gesturing so wildly in that tight, close space that we in the front row were sure we'd get stepped on. Fei, Go, and I must have understood the plays as we watched them, for we spoke Javanese at the time. But not one of us remembers today exactly what the plays were about. Judging by half-remembered impressions each of us still carries, though, the plot and action were as terrifying as the props suggested. Scowling-masked characters pursued boys and girls through the fake graveyard while actors made up to look dead danced and jigged, or a pair of lovers was ripped to pieces by demons.

But the scenes which all of us remember most vividly were from a play which told the adventures of a corpseherd. Now, we long were aware through Seeti and Lammi's stories of these men who roamed the countryside in search of cadavers. Hired by the families of those who died far from home, a corpseherd made his living by returning the dead to their families for proper burial. Trekking over the island, finding dead bodies and collecting them, he herded them to their respective homes with the use of enchanted whips and spells. We'd heard of how a corpseherd might stay overnight at an inn while his cargo of bodies leaned like boards by the door of the very room he slept in, each of them holding up its face, on which was placed a piece of paper and a sprig of parsley, to keep the flies away. We'd heard stories from Rupee, the pedicab driver who courted Seeti, claiming that he actually passed a corpseherd once on a mountainous path. Driving two or three dead bodies ahead with his whip, the man, Rupee said, was whistling a strange and melancholy tune. We imagined they roamed the countryside all hours of the day and night, corpses and corpseherds, and we always washed our faces before going to bed each night, for fear we would be mistaken for a dead one and herded away.

Inside the hut we watched as our imagination was enacted. There, one of them stood, singing a lament for the plight of those who died far from home, and waving his whip over the heads of a group of grim-looking figures who hopped about stiffly upright, trembling and jostling against each other. When the play was over we walked home through the forest in a daze, stunned by the images and songs which were as frightening and haunting as they were deeply convincing. We were amazed by the power of those who could command the dead. We pitied the ones who died far away, prodigals, wanderers, or the banished. Theirs was an unnatural predicament which had to be solved by supernatural intervention. We were terrified of the possibility of even glimpsing through trees a herd of these pathetic souls bouncing along like a group of dusty bottles. We vowed never to return to see another play. But after only a few days, we would be begging Seeti and Lammi to take us again to their village where the performances were held.

In a time during which we saw little of Mu and nothing of Ba, the stories carried us. Their telling buoyed us the way our nannies' darkened figures against the cobalt-blue sky each twilight seemed buoyed by their voices in the dissipation of day, the going light of evening. After dinner, in the faraway noise of gongs and flutes and the chants of pushcart vendors, we squatted in the yard with Lammi and Seeti and Ebu, along with the servants who worked in other neighborhood homes.

They talked while they examined each other for lice, which they picked from each other's scalps and exterminated with a little crackling sound between their fingernails. Mostly young Indonesian women who worked for Chinese families, their back-and-forth relay of local hearsay inevitably included rumors of households who had been harried by ghosts and demons, or visited by benevolent spirits. Then we would plead to hear the chronicles of their villages, the lineages of their own original families who boasted shamans and warriors of amazing power, histories of bloody feuds in which gods and devils were enlisted. By the way the women spoke, we could guess these were the oldest stories they knew, stories of a time prior to their own memories. For each time one of them began, she seemed to enter a different voice, a voice far greater than her own, and as though the telling were the very ground of what was being told, the voice itself seemed to birth the stories. And though terrified by the narratives in which religion and superstition had not yet been divorced, tales of origin and metamorphoses, we were gripped by the saying of them. And even more than the stories themselves, it was their saying we wanted to hear; a spacious, impersonal near-singing that seemed to belong to no one, even as we felt gathered in it. By hearing that voice, we felt heard by it, as though it recognized, heard, and spoke everything we hid or could never articulate.

As I sat on the earth between Lammi's squatting legs and Go sat between Seeti's, and Tai slept in Fei's arms, while the light failed and the women's faces dissolved into complete darkness, the telling continued, and as if it came from out of no mouth, it hovered disembodied, the night's pure issue. Like the swallows and bats overhead, like the distant drums from the mosques, the telling voice was just one of the late things going home. Soon, between the faint sounds of a neighbor's radio, the clattering of utensils in other kitchens, and the voices of children in other homes, we could almost hear what they claimed to hear: persistent and plaintive, from some place deep in our house and from no place in particular, a child crying.

The ice storm continued for a few more weeks, occurring once a week, and always after we were already in bed. Sometimes we all went out onto the porch and watched the ice that fell out of nowhere, while our neighbors squatted just a few feet from our front gate and did the same. It seemed our house was being thrashed and hammered by an unseen hand. And when Fei one evening put out her hand over the railing, and a piece of ice struck her palm so hard she yelped, and found it bruised the next morning, we were sure the ice had singled us out for ridicule and destruction. And then the man appeared at our door.

Mu guessed by the man's dress that he was an Arab, and she recalled that he'd rung the bell a few weeks before. Then he had asked Mu to sell her house to him, but she assured him she had no plans to sell, and he went quietly away. Now he was here again. But when Mu turned his proposition down a second time, he shot back at her, *The falling ice will continue on you*, and before Mu

could overcome her surprise at his remark and ask him
what he had to do with it, he walked angrily away, his
slippers slapping his heels loudly. The ice continued to
fall on us, just as the man promised. We sat in its roar
and furious applause as it broke windows. It tore leaves
and the tenderest branches from the wall-climbing ivy.
It stung the unsuspecting geckos clinging to leaves and
walls and left their small bodies broken on the ground. It
destroyed the flower garden. The servants chanted
loudly and begged Mu to summon a conjurer or magician. Otherwise, they would not be able to stay with us.

The police said they could do nothing to help us since
we could not prove the Arab man's complicity. *Consult a
magician to deal with magic,* they advised again. Mu began to ask around the neighborhood about the Arab.
One evening we saw him walking in our yard as if he already owned it, shaking his head, kicking at the ruined
flowers. She walked out to him and they talked. Mu understood through experience that there was no law to
which she might turn for aid, justice, or comfort. The
country had become impossible for her to inhabit. She
and the man settled on a fair price. *I'm not a robber, dear
lady,* he said. We moved out within a few days. When we
left, Mu's house looked as if something had been eating
it. Mu herself looked gnawed. She was growing lighter.
We were afraid she might disappear.

It seems strange to me now to think that many years
after we'd left Java, when my mother had the chance to
tell this story in the United States, she stood before hundreds of others like herself, refugees and immigrants,

and spoke about the mysterious hand of God which had preserved us and protected us throughout our trial in Indonesia. And after she spoke, one after another member of the Ambassadors for Christ stood up and recounted similar tribulations, each person crediting God for his or her survival. What I recall most about those meetings was the fact that all the boys and everybody's uncle at Camp Wabana seemed to be in love with Philadelphia Wong. To see that black-eyed sixteen-year-old girl walk by like a fresh-cut stem was to believe you might make it through the whole two weeks of the Ambassadors for Christ Chinese Camp and Revival Retreat.

Each year, when I was a boy, the retreat called together over four hundred members of the Ambassadors Temple to meet in a Maryland wood, where they witnessed, sang, prayed, preached, danced in the aisles, got slain in the spirit, rolled on the floor, and got generally all over holy, shouting hallelujah! My father was not officially an Ambassador, but came as an honored guest because of what was commonly referred to as his life as a living testimony of Grace. He could preach. And I'm not comparing him to the Milquetoast on TV. Nobody's seen preaching until they've seen a Chinese preacher. With his white congregation in Pennsylvania, he was toned down, even polite. And still they called him *Our heathen minister*. But in these woods of Maryland, all the fiery hollerers came, the crazy sayers and shouters, great talkers and speakers of Chinese in every imaginable dialect.

I dreamed those starry nights at Wabana that every tree closeted a man standing in silent prayer while the woods filled with Chinese-speaking wolves. When I touched my face with my paw, the fur terrorized me awake, to find myself in a room of sleeping boys, five of the older ones huddled around a lamp, arguing in whispers about Philadelphia, and outside, the faint voices of the late singers.

That so many ministers and their families gathered for two weeks meant sweaty preaching and tearful witnessing deep into the nights, cold baptisms in the lake at dawn, and soulful trembling and rocking while singing hymn after hymn of the Cross, refrain after refrain, the song leader encouraging, *Once more!* And amidst all that, Philadelphia.

So, naturally, when she was seen talking to two white boys at the lake, everyone's heart sank, thinking she was one of those who spurned their own kind. Of course, everyone was to some extent right, she was. She pretended to not be able to speak Chinese. She pretended to not know how to eat black eggs with sugar and sesame seeds sprinkled on top. But so everyone is. For a while, we all are, and then we find our kind again and love them. If we're lucky.

Philadelphia's brother, Theopholus, said of his sister, *Forget her.* But who could? With a name like Philadelphia, it hardly mattered to me who she was or what she looked like. It was the name I loved. I hardly remember what she looked like. Though I stared at her in the mess hall at breakfast like all the other boys while, one after another, three ministers offered grace. It took twenty minutes. No less than three ministers were required to bless our breakfast every morning, each one in grander fashion than the previous, each getting up and standing before that wide plain of tables and a sea of bowed heads, hungry believers, tired from the previous night's sermons and hymns. And each squeezed shut his eyes, lifted up the hands, and boomed over everybody's heads the grace, while noises from the kitchen came constant, steady, hands of women and men busying pans and utensils.

Grace was no polite affair for the Ambassadors, and the women yelled louder and heaved harder than the men. While the ministers intoned, the ministered unto did their part of the blessing, shouting *Amen!* and *Yes!* or, like a hall full of crazed giant Chinese snakes rocking back and forth in their hard plastic chairs mumbling *Yesyesyesyesyes.* Invariably, someone's arms flew up and a shout was raised: *Say it again!* And the sayer of grace started again. So it went, even while some of us began to eat.

I ate with my brothers Go and Be and our friend Theo at a big round table of other ministers' children. We liked Theo because, like us, his English had a Chinese accent. Most of the others our age had managed to refine their talk of any awkwardnesses that came from saying English with a Chinese mouth. But Theo's parents, like our own, spoke only Chinese to their children, so all we heard, except in school, was Chinese. Hence, while our vocabulary was equal to that of native English speakers, our syllables often sounded off-key. Thus, the strangeness promised by our alien faces was fulfilled in our strange-sounding speech. Acutely aware of this, we would not care in a group of Chinese, except that the Chinese without accents treated us as if we were fresh off the boat. In fact, we were only five years off the boat. And that qualified our father as a fresh witness. I was twelve, Go fourteen, and Be nine. And we, like everyone, chose our friends by how they talked, what sounded friendly. Of course, we would all feel more comfortable speaking Chinese, but we couldn't speak Theo's dialect, and he didn't speak ours, so we resorted to English. But more important, English cleaved us from our parents, who were, we believed, like parents all over the world, an embarrassment to their children.

I noticed how the conversation among the adults at our table was very much like the conversations of my parents and their friends.

"We were certain you'd all died."

"Of course, no one thought they would survive."

"We wrote so many letters on your behalf."

"Yes, I later found that out."

"Why didn't you come to Formosa when you had the chance?"

"You know my husband, how he felt about the Nationalists."

Once, my father's brother visited us in Pennsylvania with his wife and six children. The house was full of laughing and yelling and running up and down the stairs, and after huge meals of great delicacies, we cleared the table and my father played his accordion while everyone sang. Later, when the children went off to bed, the adults sat around the kitchen table and talked, sometimes until dawn. In our upstairs bedroom, crowded with cousins and siblings, Fei told softly her stories, but I could hear the voices from downstairs coming up through the heating register. One ear listening to my sister in the room, and one ear to the voices under me, I fell asleep. Sometimes I woke and everyone in the room was snoring while the voices of the adults continued from downstairs: it was all talk about what had been lost, homes they'd left behind, friends who died in prison.

But in the woods in Maryland, all that loss was somehow turned into the tie that bound everyone there, at least the adults. All the stories were practically the same. Maybe that explains why they all seemed to listen so closely when my father, giving the midnight message, asked, What brings us together, Dearly Beloved? Why have we gathered here? What fragrance has the night in store? What is a seed, Dearly Beloved? Is a fish not seed? May we not split a seed to find the fish inside? May we not open the fish to find the sea? Do the birds know what they carry? Does the day not lend us a house, the night a church? Isn't seed vanquished for the sake of seed? Doesn't winter speak a barbarous window for the sake of seed? Isn't window seed? Aren't we housed by seed, who own so little a place, such a few dust? Beloved, what is a seed? What is that bloody incandescence in a woolly shop? What we usher naked, dies into our first world. What is that we hold? What is it that ravishes us but milky seed? Our souls' rooms stretched to bursting, accommodating privilege of creation at a taxed spine. Seed in a human closet. Dearly Beloved, what is seed? Look. See how narrow the space seed keeps. Yet, how vast the house inside. And the way intricacies of hand-tooled jambs and lintels might stall and amazed us at temple thresholds in a provincial capital in China, it's easy to linger, collect on a petal at a sill of dew, and die by noon in time, and never see in what small, dark earthen jars the sacred honey sits, among the offerings of rice, fruit, salt, and burning punk. How narrow the road into the seed. How vast the house inside. How still, and how like thunder the news from inside. And if we're very quiet, Dearly Beloved, we can hear the sun there. If we close our eyes, O the rooms! And coincident with every window is a further seed, planted in the sill. While the basement holds the elder stars, and a drowned miscellany of eyeglasses and histories, teaspoons and wintry chronicles of our human arrogance. In one upper room the men sew the linen the women fold in another room, and a body lying at the top of a stairs, like a thundercloud stranded over my parched forehead, starts me doing a strange arithmetic, before I even note the first step's swept, blank as a sugar cube.

The second step, Woman, is blue.

The Roman numeral three is an Italian portico for little ancients. Or for the ants, who are more practical. They carry the day to the nth. They make a fluctuating, black-beaded line of simultaneous coming and going from here to there where the body lies, growing redolent. At the ceiling of my skull attic, a wasp nest hangs. Under

the winged seed

the nest three Chinese old women with broken feet in black cloth shoes sweep the dust and find no floor.

This is the fourth step. These are the steps I step, the going I make, a chair strapped to my back.

On the fifth I smell fried salted fish, and meet a crooked old man carrying a suitcase of left-handed scissors. He is about to speak, but I jump to the sixth, where my grandmother is stirring a soup of ginger, young hen, lemon grass, and tom yum, standing over a fire-blackened pot and crying, *Memory is salt. Don't forget me.*

On these stairs, there is no stopping, only proceedings and turnings. And there is no going back; my stepping destroys the stairs. But there are echoes on these stairs. Someone lives here. There are ashes to prove it. See the paper clips for binding. There is a tray of pencils for burning, and on a white page, something scripted in the half life of graphite. See the handscript.

And since I know now I proceed by annihilation, the constant revelation of a self-enclosed quarrel, heart the only compass and the needle wild, my voice a disintegrating text, it comes as no surprise when I reach the eleventh step dreaming of the tenth, on which I paused, recalling something my father said. The night is an indoor sea, he claimed. Man is a seed, asleep unless the lightning kills him once. And then he may surrender, and enter the grape, where a ladder of dew drops him into wine, the wafer resolved into edible flesh. Ponder this jar of blood, child, don't cry. Your right hand might as well be wood, a claw washed up on the shore between night and the unwritten, if it isn't a thief. If it isn't a

thief, kill it. For only the thief knows the way, the path
of the empty hand into the fortified seed, where the
bride waits. The hand might as well be just dumb flesh if
it isn't a baker. If it isn't a baker, send it to the kitchen,
where the companion waits, who builds the spine of
bread. Only the baker knows that bread is a form of our
deepest human wish, a shape of love. Did you think your
father was alone in the church kitchen those mornings?

Look again and see the companion, a dark patience
with a body like a standing river, and see how breaches
made in winter change to arrival; and adjustments of our
human alum to wholer soul, daily bread. Without
model, the companion bakes, the recipe in hand and
rough sack, the muscles speaking from the kneading
palm to a rocking heel, building the spine of dough, a
bound dust. Did you think it was your father alone? Love
is a massive compass and several gravity, numen manifest in what can be eaten. Know how bread is knit by
salt. For tears alone are active seed, leavening perishing
forms, apparent at an imperishable wheel of hunger. The
abundant staff is beyond every note, and only a figured
bread, designed at heart to feed an unrevealed design to
numbers of a redundant body and one equal dung, my
house, this soft brick left at the tail end of things, keeping the squeamish away by holding forth on death, with-
holding for the serious souls pronouncements of the end
of dying if we can let go of even this lump, world moved
through deep rumblings and unseen machinations of
the body's soft, obdurate parts. For shit's boon too, result
of stomach, a self, and rank fire threshing bonds and

forcing matter through base great changes, changing eaten stuff to life and death to be shat out in hot lumps looking nothing like us, yet, so us, utterly. And that smell in the air is what but dying? Nothing but perfume. Let us be singing the body passed out of the body, the evicted self, flesh of waste, for we are up from fire and straight to ashes. Where better for seeds than a residence of dung? Where better for flowers to be springing all but their secret: The dreamt color. Where is our true bed but this aromatic bread? We are bread. We should, like bread, be rising singing and, unlike bread, be knowing singing's ground, the tongue stuck in a cave of the cave-ridden, hive-laden, pitted, pocked body which shits itself, blind or disillusioned. The tongue, roughed up from shit, utters good vapors into magnificat. The sacrament is excrement, the true host is earth, peeled from us who are our guts and their furnace which make of impersonal bounties our Personhoods. Shit's what gets turned up. So here are the leaves I ate, and here are the cows. Here are the languages I speak and here are my acts. Here are my own dreamt colors, here is a blighted form, a bed I make on a heap scandalous to nostrils and intellect: death, toxic to logic, now acknowledged, the object, my thought. Here is what was promised, earth, ultimatum and limit, tactless, tacit, our rough draft and true contract, shit and desire alive in unstable dialectic, here is your destiny, manifest, and only slowly transacted to fire, to fire, to fire, and then to bread, could so more slowly go to seed the word. Did I think we were alone in our human kitchen? Bread is the altered air, adjusted earth, in turn adjusted by a superabundant sun. Anyone's widest orbit equals only himself. Did I think I was alone? No one merely kneads any wheat with water, the way is remembrance to the one whose hands are had by love's cold ache, suffering the adjustable flesh. For the finite is sanctified only by an infinite resign. Resign now the bowl, alabaster. Prepare now the body, wasted nard. Make true bread, a feeding flesh, a speaking ear.

And then he set out on an unnumbered wave and, being right-handed, pulled his boat opposite the clock, which reads 5:04 A.M. And as long as my father rows ahead of me, there can be no place. Place there is none. And rest is the interval between my woman's eyes, or my dark hammock slung between her and China, where I walked once after dark, and stepped into a clue the roses were leaving, for I was in the city of roses, Tientsin. So I stood there a while, the perfume fanned gently by bicycles passing from dark to dark. A while ago, I wept in my dream like a heartbroken child for my father's shoes, and now I see there is no boat abandoned that the sea does not take back, haft to haft, and every gunwale, board, nail, each shape of departure Chinese boatbuilders I come from planed into the timbers.

So night eventually moves over. As long as my father rows. And no sooner do I think I know the name of his boat or the shape this hour will take, a shadow darkens the throat of the chalice in which one hand is moving over an open face to divine a countenance. And depending on which way I traveled behind my father, with or without a destiny, as ambassador or refugee, the

rain blew across our sleep or down on our backs, and
neither of us was sure if I was growing taller in his doorway, or if he was walking farther than I could follow.
Since he rows, both have become true. So I go out to
meet him, taller than he remembers, and much older.
And if I come to a bare place, I change my life and
every increment of the sun to a further flower, three-
fold. And already the night enlists, while my stepping
unwrites the steps, to make my entrance sheer. On the
stairs, even my ear is a corpse, a dead little cartilage,
and I have to hear with the close-cut stem, the green-
blue nexus, barely ear, for there is the eye about it;
therefore call it the seeing stem, but not a thinking
reed. Call it a green waist, this listening; a living seam
and habitation in the air, though now the wound is
closing between my legs.

What was a luxurious trench and fiery head, is now
withdrawn, less than a little mouse in a nest of black
hair. Oh, to be touched, Woman, to have the wound
open, awake, fresh to desire, the seeds ganging the
wounded stalk, the blood seen under the skin. To be
wounded over and over by you, long and long, to be
honing the very edges of the afflicted meat by loving, to
enter your wound with my own. When what's inside us is
outside, when what was secret emerges from its fleshy
hood and labial veils and, being seen, sees, when we are
drawn each to each, then we wed in the flesh, in the
only body we ever had. That bright sensation of blood,
that humming along the length of the wound, that di-

vining of you of me-in-you, that driving at the pit of you, is the blood seeing. Desire is the wound knowing you, and thereby knowing itself.

But it is closed now. Between my legs, blood unseen and unseeing. My body is so alone of you, Girl, my body unverified by you, like those statues we saw when we visited that old capital city in China. Remember, my love, how hard it was to get there. Remember how poor and friendly the people were on the train, how they promised they would tell you when we passed the Yellow River, and when we finally did one evening, the whole carload yelled out *Yellow River!* and there alongside the train, in the dusk-blackened land, gleamed one thin winding band of water. Remember the night we arrived at our destination, the old capital, how shocked we were the next morning to discover in daylight a city quite different from the one we came to at night. It was in that city, at the grave of a famous king, we saw, in a stadium-size excavated pit, the hundreds of life-size funerary statues of soldiers. Some of them stood whole and wholly uncovered. Others lay shattered, or stood broken. Still others were left in various stages of unearthing, as though caught in the process of emergence, human shapes figuring out of dirt; a nose, an extended hand, a knee, a forehead. Sometimes just the front of a soldier's face and body appeared, seeming to march out of the earthen walls. Or march into the earth, when only the back was exposed, as you sleep now your lithe dark sleep.

They may be open, but my eyes see nothing, so they

don't even know their own looking. Two stones in their skull sockets. I should open a window. I'd do it but I'd have to get up and that might wake you. So I lie here scribbling words. I lie on my back scribbling pages of words which, in the morning, only I can read, the cursive running at odd angles, the letters spread into illegibility, looking like mad graphs of a crazy heart.

Your body is near me. But there is another. Is there another?

Who's here? I'm here. You're here.

Who else is here? No one. Here, as in childhood, there is no one but me, and nothing but the right hand, writing what the left hand erases, laying to waste the dark for want of you. The right hand should have been a bird, and the left hand flying under it for a shadow. Or give the foot its job. It's obvious the foot has always wanted to be a hand. And might as well let the heart be its own rich liver, while we're at it, and liver a liquid gold. But what would we do with love, then? I say restore it to its rightful proportion, its very origin, the sun. But

then, I'm just a mouth, which is itself nothing but a talk-

ing ear, and a talking ear a listening wound, a trumpet,

almost God. And if at this point there approaches out of

the East a man with a stone tangled in his hair, and he

asks you what you did with your father's blind eye, that

agate, unblinking, what will you say?

How will you answer the questions morning begins to

pose? Who appointed the birds secretary to the grass?

Who licensed the wind? If I sit here long enough, will

winter make a house in my right knee? Will anyone

come to lead me home? Where is East? Now that my fa-

ther's dead, and my mother's old (she who sits alone in

her living room and waits all afternoon for me to visit)

who will call me? And by what name? What name, what

one word, might contain me, who are one, yes, yet le-

gion, various as the hand-colored stones my sister

painted when we were children, my heart myriad as her

hair? Mustn't each one fix his own sign? What's mine?

the winged seed

I'M WAITING FOR my father, and the clock says I have hours before day. Here, as in childhood, it is the same solitude. Here as in childhood, I practice my Chinese, writing right to left, while my mother walks back and forth saying the words I write. My father's name was *Perfect Country*, which I write by drawing a spear enclosed in a heart and piercing the heart from within. My mother's name is *House of Courage*, and as she paces back and forth, uttering, as my grandmother's cane taps past the window, down the redbrick path, my head bends to the task, making the pictures that are the words my mother says, the words which are the pictures of the infinite versions of the insect sun. Here, as in childhood, it is the same, I make the strokes and say the sounds to myself; say *jia* for *home*, and put the pig under a roof (家); say *heng* for *constancy*, and set the boat adrift (恒); I stand the bearded wheat to the right of an el-

der ear. I plot the progress of the seed into summer and
innumerable leaves, and set a three-spoked wheel beside
the lotus; I give you morning glory. I let two birds descend to braid the lightning; I write my father's name,
Perfect Country (国); I write my mother's, *House of
Courage* (家). I make the sign for *what*
(么), for *who* (谁), and *again* ( ); here as in
childhood, I count the cloves of *fire* under *horse* ( ).
While Auntie naps in her room, the *China Daily* unread
on the floor, I do four strokes for *six*, and eight for *that*.
While the fan in the parlor churns the breathed air to
disturb the daylilies a little. I fill the page, with picture
after picture for *scarab*. I make a hand issuing out of a
cloud, I make the little rain. I mix memory and forget-
ting, I hurry shadows, while holding noon at a standstill.
And news from my mother's garden is the wind unsorts
the roses, looking for someone, while I let a hand hover
above the darkened wine, while I hunt the picture that's
my name, and make a woman carry a blind sheaf on her

head, a furrow of waves arriving perpetually, while I look for something to keep, something the wind won't eventually inherit, the sun disperse, time unravel. I look for a word, one word which said is a picture. I look for a pictured word. For a word is a kind of commitment and, depending on which hand you heed, left or right, or the palm standing open in that cave we call the heart, the naked hand among lions and weasels, the hand exposed to the heart's briny, pregnant salts and murderous blood, good blood for sausage, the right hand which writes to its brother, the left, to say, Brother, forgive my claw. My cloven foot, and my feathers where the lice are at home. I forgive the perfume with which your letters come, yesterday to tell of one cold blossom opening outside our father's window. And I forgive your pale face, your hairless foot, so frightening to me when we were boys. I forgive you the scar on my forehead. I forgive your left hand the stone. I forgive your left-handed heart its poor purse. Forgive my jaw its bone, my belly its unanimous hunger, enough for both of us. I hope you like the black seeds I enclose. They are odorless. They lie very still. I hope you like them. Look at them and think of me, your brother.

Depending on which hand writes, I said, a word is a possible body. So I filled square after square of the sheets of blue grid my mother placed before me as a child, page after page, I copied her hand, making the signs for *lily* (合 花), *wicker* (藤), *paper bird* (纸 鸟); I set the *moon* under a hill, put *sun* above *is,* an *eye* below *front, right* next to *present.* Here, as in childhood, I read backward and forward, sweeping the leaves with my left hand, and sorting the needles with my right, while my mother's fountain asks, *What's your name?*

Here, as in childhood, I grow old alone before the empty pages, practicing my mother's Chinese at my mother's table. I remember how the difficult wilderness gleamed beneath my hands, all that hard, dark rosewood of my inheritance, polished to bright knock and no entrance. I still see that boy. Awake before dawn, the light hours away, he sat reading out loud the book of Numbers or Deuteronomy, swinging his legs back and forth, suspended between the separate woods of table and floor when suddenly his voice grew foreign to him, and he became lost. He couldn't speak. Couldn't call out for fear his voice might walk away and return to him a stranger, with questions he can't answer, invitations he must keep. And so, pinned to an odd height from the ceiling and stranded at an immeasurable distance from the floor, he turned the flightless pages of his book. And if we think he is terrified, he is. But we must not wish for him the terror to pass too soon. Nor his hunger. For he has finally arrived by himself to where no one else could take him, and where no story will save him, O Mother, today I am what is least inside you: tomorrow. Tomorrow, I'm my father's son. Today a black seed who loves Christ, bald seed, black Christ, O Mother, today! Today you house me and I keep you, your strongest knight, bow and arrow, your narrowest hour, two of my three sides finned, a winged seed! Dear Mother, I'm what you never thought to own, I'm yours, yours twice, and smaller. O my sister, I'm near you, your ache, and you can't sleep. I'm in you, the last and therefore next and heretofore uncried salt. And you must cry me, your brother. O Lover, Donna, let me be what is least in you: dusk. From which our journey starts without announcement, two doves flushed from my father's unmown field!

Here as in childhood, a visitor waits for me. At the back door, under the lintel-ivy, he extends a hand to hand me a note on which is written my name, which becomes my mission. Here as in childhood, no one knows me, and I make the strokes, stroke after stroke, *run* under *stars* and *two* coming through the *trees*, sun behind sun for eternity. I write a lintel, and make the upper and lower signs, and three times draw the character for *sun* (日 日 日), and repeat, *r, r, r!* the sun! the sun! the sun! the Great Navel! *R* for the sun, pouring mouth, unquenchable lion, blank gate, wheel. Therefore I declare a new period, the sun, our ultimate orient, ninety-nine golden bicycles wheeling, spire ongoing, gyre. With R, all things become possible. R lit out and I lit out after R! R walked into a walled garden and I did not follow, but slept across the threshold; and therefore, this morning, I come to collect on a petal, at the sill of dew, and must die by noon in time. R has the balm. R is a dread digitalis. Find R. R is complete. R takes aim from ninety-three million miles, and fires along our blue mantle the ten thousand flowers and fires we live and die by. Does it have a period? Is True North East, and past our indoor sea? Aren't I the last man from China? Aren't I the first? And mustn't I surrender to my eventual Easter? That makes R a third-handed man. But R is a bird, so R will be flying. The tool is in my hip pocket, but the balm's in R's hold, is even R's very property, who is without property, hemless, suggesting infinitely R.

One day, I was waiting for R at a wall, among the other dead leaves, and suddenly heard the sweeping, and knew it was time, me in R's wake, at a crest, in peril, about to get swept. Why did I come here? For R. But R's not here. The widow said R just left. The sun must have been in your eyes, she said. It happens all the time. You look for R in the sun, where you thought you buried him, and he walks right by, a self-erasing signature in occluded time. Here, the widow said, he left you this, then handed me a folded note. Now don't hang around here leaning on the roses. So I left, while she went on sweeping.

And now where will I go? Where might R be? What is that smell? Last night the incense tree was burning.

They say there's always a man caught in the branches, but I didn't see him. Is it left to me to ask the birds after R? The birds pass the secret among them. The birds can't help here. Shall I open the note the widow handed me and read the question written in R's hand? *What is the work of love?* R lit out again.

Before R touched me, I touched myself. After R, no other hand could make me cry out as though I were dark harbor to nothing but seagoing birds that prey on maternal silence in order to proclaim a many-beaked and ·taloned appetite to foam and white jet. The very night R parts with R's darker night is a dead swoon. I may have been killed by R for R's sake, I don't know. R is such teeth, so much veil, pink, and all black, black, black. Black R. Invisible waist at which I keep arriving.

But I knew of R before R came and knew me. As water was troubled by a woman's hair long before I came down with my father to the Solo River, where each of us washed his seamless garment, while things we said and things we did not say, like equal halves of the oyster shell, opened to reveal our common unassayable nacre, and a single wisdom: R is manifold, and no one may know R, and already October's leaves make room for R; already, this morning is moving over for unfurnished noon, and the empty house I lived in as a child by the Solo; a house no more a house, and one day cleared of furniture by soldiers, and a young lieutenant in a too-big uniform waving a stack of papers bearing the red rubric of the latest president. How odd it was to be left only a clock. Our mother wept into a white hand.

How would we live in all those empty rooms? With our mother at the prison so much visiting our father, our days had already come to seem like vacant reaches, mute hours absent of Ba and Mu. How did we become so small and our house so empty? We flew through the rooms, casting our voices everywhere, only to have them returned, doubly hollow. And every day the house grew bigger, until it seemed the very precinct of daylight. We lived with the no-longer-there, and the drastic removal of Ba, and the gradual going of Mu. A corner where a couch used to brood was so blank, to stand in that spot was to feel almost transparent. And to stand in the middle of the dining room where the six-legged rosewood hulk used to preside was to wobble as a slender axis about which a massive vacuum revolved. But, resilient children for whom everything seemed an adventure, we grew daily more accustomed to our lot. We made our days out of nothing but waiting. We invented games. In a game called *Come find us* a blindfolded one sought her hidden siblings. But there were too few places to hide in an empty house, so we relied on silence and stillness to help us escape detection.

How strange a game it is, and how dark, when the seeker is both sought and fled, the object not so much to outwit the seeker as it is to master your own impatience, which often forced you, after only a few moments of hiding, to walk directly into the seeker's path, in order to have done with the waiting. That we mustn't do. The best way to win the game was to find a place to sit down and stop playing. Restlessness betrayed you those after-

noons. An infinite repose won. Forget the one who
moved in search of you, now closer and even closer, now
farther. The way R moves even now, looking for you.
Forget the one, blindfolded, alone and full of her own in-
audible singing, who sought to touch you. And nobody's
part in the game was more difficult than the seeker's,
who had to bear not only the solitude of one alone, but
the terror of the stranded. Do not ask if it's R feeling her
way down one hall and another, in and out of one room
and the next, for it might be you whose any sense of
where you are fails you, and every wall becomes another
your hands multiply, each corner the same corner. In
those instances, you will be reeling in a confusion verg-
ing on panic, and you are perfectly lost. While to the
waiting one, the rooms seem immense. The door to the
courtyard, and the other to the hallway, seem unfamiliar,
as though you never knew what lay on the other side,
just as everything suddenly looked strange to me, who
sat, waiting to be found in an empty room. The feeling
was the same as when I sometimes wakened from a nap
to find myself in an alien afternoon, a strange bed, while
beyond the mosquito net someone I seemed to know
once, reading in a chair by the window, lifts his head
when there falls through the open shutters the plumed
cry of an island bird, a nearly human shuttle, a calling toward unfathomable distance from the East, where, if I
look now, I see rising, a new form of East, though man or
fire, clay or tree, R or what, who could say?

But I put off my shoes to meet it. I close my eyes to
drink that good water, distillate of time and R. That

makes me, I suppose, the last man from China. Or the first. Or one of the dying. I can't remember which. As the last, you might say I wake every morning and climb a murderous stair into the sun to harvest black seeds there, in order to find my eye of the eternal audience, impersonal R. As the first, you might say I'm the last, and I surrender to the next, my Easter. As one of the dying, however, I dream continually of houses, time assembled in space, mansions of our possible hours, and hours on porches letting onto days. I gather furniture, galleries of couches and armchairs. French doors and circular portals to Chinese gardens where mute shadows mingle with the sleep of presidential grandfathers and grandmothers. Houses I knew and houses I did not.

When Ba was a boy, he lived in an old, falling-down, two-story house that must have once been beautiful with its carved balustrades, and red tile roof, the edges of the flared eaves encrusted with ceramic figures. By the time he was born, though, the place, long neglected, was nothing but a creaky-staired hull of flaking paint and broken trim, with grass and little trees sprouting in the cracked brick courtyard, and so many empty rooms he couldn't imagine what they were for, and none of them heated in winter. He lived with his mother, a sister, and a brother in a few rooms at the front of the building, while the rooms at the back stood abandoned. All of them but two, in which his grandmother and her brother lived, the old woman seldom showing her face for fear of seeing her son, and the old man confined by locks and chains. Ba's father lived with them a few days a week in

l
i
•
y
o
u
n
g

l
e
e

that house in the countryside outside Peking and kept an apartment in the city, where he did most of his work.

His family had been wealthy for a long time, establishing their money in the fishing industry, but most of the money had long been squandered and badly invested when Ba's father was old enough to wish it weren't so. He ended up with only the house when his father died. His mother was left owning a match factory which she had no idea how to run, and which Ba's father would inherit when she died. Ba's father made his living traveling as a broker in antiques and precious stones. By guile, charm, and good looks, and the knack for singling out suckers and first-time buyers and sellers, he not only swindled amazing sums of money but ended up amassing a decent collection of antiques.

Of course, his reputation spread, and he could not count on working in the same area for very long. So he traveled, and in the meantime, he bought a car and chauffeur, tailored European suits and hats, and visited America and Indonesia two or three times. But even as his family watched him get richer, not much changed for them, though they listened to his plans and promises to change their wretched lives. The house remained derelict, unheated in fall and winter. The ceilings leaked during rain. He was gone most of the time and never left them food or money.

I don't know how he thought we were surviving, Ba told me, as I bathed him one day, the body I became custodian to when I turned eighteen, after his fourth heart attack. Once a week I lifted Ba from his dying-bed, stripped him, and put him in the water.

My grandmother supported us with the diminishing profits from the factory. In fact, when my father was gone, we got to eat, while when he was home we starved. For he considered our eating a lack of filial piety. We were to defer to him in everything. I listened, I soaped his bony shoulders and his skinny neck where the collarbones jutted hugely their knuckles. I lifted his arm and soaped its pale, flaccid length, and then the ribs, where R feasted. *And since any food put in our mouths was looked upon as food taken out of his, our times with him resembled a strange kind of playacting. After the maid had set the food on the table, plates and plates of deliciously prepared meats and vegetables, my father would smile and ask, his voice full of merriment, "Shall we eat?" and we had to answer, "No thank you, Father, we've eaten." Then he would act genuinely surprised, even though it was the same routine each time, and he'd ask, "Eaten? Are you sure? Why not have a bite with your father?" At which we were to insist, "No thank you, Father. We're too full, but you should go ahead and enjoy yourself."*

The shoulder blades, as I glided my hand over them, seemed like hinges where old wings might have once been jointed. I noticed again the bloated feet and the missing toenails. I recalled his telling me when I was a boy how he'd lost his toenails in prison, but that was another story. Here, my father was telling me how his father ate with relish while his family watched, starved and yearning for just one taste of anything on the table. And while he ate, he thanked out loud the gods for the

l i • y o u n g l e e

blessing of children with such a deep sense of honor and love for the patriarch. My father's mother, who also participated in the farce, sat opposite her husband at the long table, smiling, starving, and agreeing aloud with him. The leftovers, as a rule, were thrown in the garbage, which the patriarch inspected himself to make sure, he claimed, that none of his beloved family should eat food that had been left out too long. So they were happy to see him go on his business trips. When he stayed at home longer than three days they barely survived. For only in secret did they live on the food the grandmother bought and her maid prepared. Once, when Ba's father found out that his wife and children were eating, he beat them all with a stick, screaming like a madman, *Do I not provide for you that you should eat from another's kindness?* while the woman and the children begged his forgiveness and apologized over and over.

Even his own mother was afraid of him. And when she found out that he was planning to murder her in order to speed his inheriting the match factory, she signed the whole thing over to him on the spot. He turned right around and sold it for a huge profit, and then the family moved to Tientsin, where no one had heard of him, for his name had become, as they say, like the smell of dog shit on your shoes.

In the city, it wouldn't do for them to live the way they had been living in the past. They had to appear respectable. Besides, he discovered that his daughter and son might be assets to his social life and his business with their rapidly improving English and the young girl's beauty and natural social graces. A business-minded man, he invested in this and that and was always lucky. He began taking his children everywhere with him, to lunches and parties where he cruised like a grinning fish for potential victims. Soon, they moved into the French district of the city, into a house near the huge complex of buildings which housed the Yuan clan. There, my father began to court the oldest granddaughter of the fifth wife of Yuan Shih-k'ai, warlord to the Dowager Empress during the twilight of the dynasty.

Finished bathing him, I gather him in my arms and lift his loose and dangling frame out of the water to set it down in a chair I'd covered with a bath towel, but though his white skin seems a mere web, loosely draped to connect bones that poke and protrude, he's surprisingly heavy. I barely manage to lift him out of the water, and not without knocking a knobby knee or brittle anklebone against the white tub. I'm practically wrestling him, and he's gripping the sides of the tub, reaching for a nearby towel bar. My fear is he'll fall apart in my arms like a puzzle and I'll never get him put together. I fear I've dislocated something, he groans so. The bathroom floor is wet and slippery, my clothes are soaked, and I know that the warm bath has stirred his bowels, but he can't move them without my aid, and I will have to do what I've done all the other times. I'll dry the floor while he sits in the chair, and then I'll lay a towel I've warmed on the heater across the floor, and put him on it, lying on his side. I'll pull a surgical glove over my right hand

and enter him from behind to dig out the hard lumps of shit while he groans and pants.

My body is Ba's body, the same. But my dying is all my own, though nothing compared with the dying Ba did before our very eyes. Ba's dying was like a bitter wand snapped off a huge tree of dying. It possessed a magical concentration of death. It drew everyone in the house to watch it. So everyone fled who was able, the way one rows from a sinking ship to be a safe distance away from the immense going down. He lay huge on his bed, bones jutting, prehistoric, and mumbled words about the price of knowing R intimately. R was in the hipbones sitting like archaeological specimens on the mattress. R was being revealed to me in the sore-infested body, the slack skin, and bulged, swollen joints of dying Ba, in the ribs and their grinning. R resided in the shadows gnawing Ba's face to strangeness. R was at rest in Ba's decaying flesh. R grinned in his ribs. Naturally, I began to believe that if I was to reveal R, as Ba said I must, if I was to be an instrument of a greatest disclosure, it would necessarily mean my getting erased. I wasn't sure if I could pay such a price. And I wondered what, then, was the reason for my own body, or the body of Mu, in its soft, diaphanous flesh. But there it was before me, day after day, Ba's downfall and R's gradual evidencing. No part of me resisted Ba's body, which took on greater weight as it wasted. In its disappearing, it grew ever more present. His going away was larger than any body or fellowship of bodies drawn to his bedside. Ba's vanishing was R's becoming, heralded by Ba's own becoming entirely

t
h
e

w
i
n
g
e
d

s
e
e
d

unrecognizable to anyone who knew him.

I remember on the day he died, a spider came out of hiding from under a serrated leaf, and clung to the bouquet which my love bore in her naked arms to me, both her arms pricked and stabbed, her face cut, her eyes within inches of the thorns, my love-among-the-thorns, Donna Lee, among serrations and edges, her eyes closed to elude the green points, her lightly feathered arm scourged for my love of roses.

When *R* was a spider, *R* rode on a thorn in a treacherous bouquet which, set on the dining-room table, looked like a giant nest, the great eagle's perhaps, that inhabiter of horned regions, the dweller of great hours. Her white hat, set beside it on the dark rosewood, looked like a big camellia.

When *R* was a spider *R* was grayish green, his head smaller than his abdomen. I saw him leap off his thorn and walk lightly the length of a maiden's arm, and jump to the table and, on all its toes, proceed over its reflection to the end of the world, where, on the day I die, I will be wondering, How will I know *R* when I find *R*? Will my fingers waken when I move them over *R*? Will they know what they touch and tell me so? They cling so briefly to any knowledge, *R* or a woman's skin, before they're dull again, unknowing. Lights go out. My fingers, dumb, they lie against your thigh, my love; they register merely the pressure of you, but nothing more. Not until I start them moving again do they waken to distinctions of your coarseness and fineness, looseness and denseness, coolness and warmth. Restless, they are awake to

you and wakened by you. Stilled, they're dumb meat.
Flesh stays awake by the freshness it wakens to. My flesh
wakens to itself by freshness of you. Otherwise, the body
is cumbersome, a crawling-off dandruff.

Now, without warning, I think I could waken to myself if you woke. That's all it would take. I can't waken. I
need you to raise me by your love. Otherwise, all of me
sleeps, a loaf of flesh and spine the consistency of a man.
But if I could exist within you, I could exist. If I could
penetrate you, I could be penetrated. Who's here on the
night I died? No one. It's just me alone wondering, Can
anyone touch himself as deeply as another might?
Where is my flower? How might I open? What have I
made of my life?

A boy who has been sitting on the floor of a dark hall
a long time outside a locked door could be listening to
the terrifying engines of sex, with hot, embarrassed ears,
or the howling of madness, terrifying, pitiful, depending
on what city he's in, Shanghai or Tientsin, and depending on if the door is locked from inside the room or out.
If it's locked from the inside that means the keys to that
door, as well as other doors to other rooms, or houses, or
safety deposit boxes, are in his father's pants, which are
most likely creased—except for the pants pocket, hung
with the weight of its cluster of keys—very neat on a
hanger in a closet of that room on the door's other side,
the lit side, where a large window takes in the afternoon
light, some of which has spilled under the door to lie, a
thin white stripe, burning beside the boy's hand, which
lies palm down next to the threshold of the room whose

interior he has never seen, for when his father comes out with his pants on, and vest and suitcoat and hat in hand as well, and stands with his back to the boy, he blocks the view of the room, stops up the light which might come pouring out into the hall, in order to say good-bye to the woman inside, who sometimes steals a glance past the man, at the boy who has been sitting in darkness, and who now rises in partial darkness, and will accompany his father down many flights of narrow stairs into daylight, then on a series of errands which will most likely end with the man making large deposits at the Bank of Shanghai.

When my father was a boy in China in the early 1930s, he squatted in the summer in the brick courtyard of the house he was born in, and watched an old servant woman chop sandalwood, then grind it into a fine powder to burn at the household shrines, one in each of the thirty-six rooms of his father's two-story house, built in the countryside a few miles outside Peking. Twice a day, she ground incense and burned it, this nameless, black-cotton-clad, toothless old soul, withered, bowlegged, and bent almost horizontal from years of hauling and carrying every manner of her master's, my grandfather's, belongings, water, coal, and children. She even carried the master himself to school and back when he was a boy. That she lived long was her curse, she sometimes told my father, the boy who watched her chop. That the master long ago had stopped finding her desirable was her only blessing. For my grandfather had been known to beat, whip, and stab with needles the servants, girls and boys, he found sexually pleasing. But the old woman survived all that, and since she was too weak to do much else, she was used to chop and burn the sandalwood, for which she received three bowls of watery porridge a day, and sometimes a soft turnip cake. When she was found dead one morning, the other servants simply rolled her stiff body up in the dirty reed mat she slept on each night, and carried her out the back door. And someone else prepared the incense. For it had to be burned twice a day and in every room. For my grandfather's single greatest fear all his life was madness, which he understood to be the work of evil gods, and which he guarded against by putting in each room a shrine to a god or dead ancestor. Years later, in another house, he continued the practice, but instead of a dead ancestor here and there, a Buddha or an elephant god, he dedicated all the shrines to Jesus. For extra protection, sundry charms and tassels, various Daoist charts and symbols were hung on door jambs, over mirrors, and inside closets.

It wasn't unreasonable that he feared madness, for along with the house and fortune which fell to him when his father died, my grandfather inherited the responsibility of an insane uncle. In fact, his own father had died mad, chained to a four-poster bed, his mind ravaged by syphilis. The presence of his uncle was a constant burden to him. The crazed man was kept locked in one of the rooms at the back of the house, where my father was sent when he was punished.

The door to the brothel room closes with a neat click, unlike the sound of tomb doors or the foot-thick oak door to another room the boy has sat outside of often enough, for an hour or hours, depending on the sentence, contingent upon the crime, which could be anything from stripping a leaf of the newly planted bamboo in the garden, to smudging the chauffeured Packard's window with hair grease when the boy falls asleep on the long ride home, either of which acts of boyish thoughtlessness could get him sentenced to sitting outside the door to a locked room, and wondering about the one kept on the other side, the one whose blood runs thickly in the boy, so thick he feels dragged down with it, and thickly in the boy's kin, and will run the same, he thinks, inside his children, who will, years from now, be continually warned by him about the blood which is loud inside them, itchy inside them, his children, whose blood will be noisy with stories about the one on the other side, insane from syphilis inherited from his fathers, on whom the blood depended, but with whom I have nothing to do, since I've disavowed them one and all, all of them I never knew, and I've disavowed those from whom they were begot, all of them I never knew, and I've disavowed all those they begat, all but one, the one who immediately preceded me in life and who precedes me now on his longest flight down a very dark hall very subterranean, a hall not entirely unlike the halls he sat in, those double tunnels, I mean; those twin lengths of equal dark, two cruel sentences, each similar to the other in enough details so as to make the two seem one, so as to make, in one boy's compulsive recollection and a second boy's obsessive reconstruction, one seem charged

with the horror of the other or the other lit with the
eeriness of the one; either way, the boy, who grew up and
married and fathered children, me among them, carried
inside him, until the day of his death, those twin shafts
of muddy light, sibling horrors among many other varied
and myriad episodes—forgotten or remembered, terrifying or beautiful—episodes which I call, arbitrarily, "his
life," as a way to get a handle on it, as a way to think
about him, which, as it turns out, is just another way to
think about myself, which I seem to do often, part of the
reason being, I'm certain, that *he* did it so much,
thought about me, that is, pointing his finger at me and
shouting You! or shaking his head and breathing as if
sick with me You! or beating me and saying You! his
meat hungry for my meat, You! seeking my meat, You!
and finding it, You! his pithy utterance coincident with
his flesh falling heavily on me, You! You! You! his flesh
meeting my stubborn flesh stubbornly, his fisted falling-
on-me making a sound only bodies meeting in rage can
make, You! and me wondering, Me? since I could not
understand what was so god-damned interesting about
Me! but he would explain, lest I remain in wonder, explain that I was killing him, while his thick palm fell fast
and much on me, that I was worthless mucus of a
woman's body, his Sunday shoes fitting deeply to me,
that I should be dead, should die, while his flesh made
bone and flesh fall on my kneeling flesh, should die!,
while his flesh sought its satisfaction, and found no satisfaction, should die! while his flesh persuaded my flesh it
should die, my flesh which he did love, did hold, some-

times, and woo, saying, You are my very liver, my flesh, my life.

I remember hiding, quiet as good mice, with Fei, Go, and our cousin Wren, under Aunt Maria's vanity, when Wren's father reached one big groping hand inside the frilly lace skirt to find one of us. I remember, as the skirt parted, noticing how the gleaming wood floor stretched the whole way to the shut door. And the big hand found Wren, it always found Wren, and yanked him out, who started to make a noise like someone about to go down a slide for the first time. I remember the chunks of diamonds set into thick gold bands on Uncle Colin's thick fingers, those fingers that looked so much like Ba's. As Wren grabbed one of the vanity's legs, trying to crawl back to our hiding place, the perfume bottles clinked and rattled overhead. The rest of us stayed absolutely still, and watched Wren get dragged to the middle of the bedroom floor. And there the rain of blows began, his father's heavy flesh falling hard and fast on Wren. Wren howled and whined, curled up while fist and foot fell everywhere on his body no bigger than Fei's. I remember the way the polished floor stretched the whole way to the shut door. I remember the shut door the whole way at the end of the gleaming floor. Just when we thought his father was through, leaving the room and slamming the door behind him, he came back and began all over again. Again he left. Again he came back. Again he was gone. We sat a long time behind the curtains of the vanity and he didn't return. We sat stupefied, filled with an inexplicable shame, and dull as to what to do. I can't remember if we looked at Wren, sobbing out there on the floor. I know I tried to think of anything else but what I'd just witnessed. I wondered where Mu was. I thought about my little brother Tai's red stool by the kitchen door at home. I remembered the way he smacked his lips and sighed after Fei gave him gulps of cherry soda. He rode Fei's good hip all day long, wanting no one else when Mu was gone. Once, when he was barely one, he'd gotten a bad cold, and Fei cleared his labored breathing with her mouth by sucking out the fluid from his nose and spitting it out. She'd learned that from my nanny, Lammi, who'd done the same for me each time I was sick. I suddenly longed for Lammi. I wondered where she was and if I'd ever see her again. I wondered if I'd ever see Ba again.

I remembered the day, it seemed ages ago, when he had showed up at the door in what looked like pajamas. He was accompanied by a prison guard he had bribed into letting him come home for a few hours. Unable to get word to Mu that he was coming, he had taken the chance that she might be home. She wasn't. She'd gone, as on every other day, to the prison. While one of the servants left to find Mu, and the guard sat in the living room drinking beer and eating snacks the cook prepared, Ba waited in hopes that Mu might get back early. He didn't talk or touch us, but sat nervously across from us in a chair in the cool dark of Mu's bedroom. After a long time sitting in the dark, he reached out his left arm and turned on the bedside lamp. He looked intently around the room a long while. Then he turned the lamp off and sat staring blankly ahead. After several minutes, he turned on the lamp again and glanced about the room again, as though he were looking for something. Then we all sat in darkness once more, all of us with blank looks on our faces. He repeated this several times until a servant came in to inform him that the guard had decided it was wise to leave. I remember how terrified we were of Ba that day. He looked, after all, different, gaunt, dark, feral. And he smelled a little. He told us to tell Mu he had been home, then, after kissing each of us, went into the bathroom and put a fresh bar of sandalwood soap in his pocket, and followed the guard away. We were almost relieved to see him go, and as he stepped through the back garden gate, Go ran to catch up with him and, yelling *Thief!* reached into his pocket and ran back to the house with the soap.

I remembered all of it while I sat under Aunt Maria's vanity. I didn't look up at Fei or Go, and they didn't look at me or one another. And none of us made a sound. Now as I think back to that day in Aunt Maria's and Uncle Colin's bedroom, I realize that that might be the first time I felt separate from Fei and Go, frighteningly so. I don't know if I was suddenly rent from them in that moment, or if I was made suddenly aware of a condition of apartness which had been true all along. Unable to lend help to Wren, proven powerless and ineffectual, I began to sense our helplessness toward each other. It was clear now that anything could happen to any one of us, and the others would have to sit silently in semidarkness and watch. And perhaps we wouldn't even watch.

Perhaps we would simply stare at our fingers, our knees, listen intently to a song inside our heads, recall our favorite food. After all, Ba was taken, and what could we do? Tai was taken, and we were kept from mourning him. Mu was gone. What could we do? Beaten and shamed, Wren lay out there alone, quiet and still now, for he'd fallen peacefully asleep. That all of us were stranded inside ourselves was a new feeling, but it would become as familiar to us as a bad habit, and then, as again and again we felt it—in that house and later in the wide world—it would take on the irrefutable constancy of a truth. We couldn't have known it then, but our lives had already begun to change in a direction which dictated we would soon leave Jakarta and spend the next twenty-five years of our lives living in other people's homes and being told which rooms we should and should not enter.

I remember now what we were doing at our aunt and uncle's house. The morning Tai woke with a fever, Mu stayed home. For two days she hovered over him while he lay in bed delirious, sometimes convulsing so violently we feared he'd snap himself in two. After three more days in the hospital, we never saw our brother again. For reasons not made clear to us, we weren't permitted to attend his funeral.

After Tai's death, Mu went away from us, we didn't know where. We were sent to Bandung to live with our uncle Colin, Ba's brother, his kind-hearted Austrian wife, Auntie Maria, and their nine children, the oldest one a year older than Fei, and all of them, to our amazement, blonde. Auntie Maria told us that Mu was resting, recovering from what had been a very trying time, and that we were having a vacation. She tended to us like her own.

But we wanted to know when we could go home. Soon, we were told, after our vacation. We wanted to know how long Mu would be gone. Not long, was the answer. And we needed to know what happened to Tai. When we asked how he had died, we were told he'd been playing with a harmonica that had been left out in the rain, had gotten sick from swallowing the rust that had formed on it, and then gotten a fever and died. For years afterward, this very story was cited each time any of us asked how our brother had died. For years I lived with a mixture of fear and fascination with rust; I would bend down to anything scribbled with it and take in that sharp, bright scent, completely convinced it was the poison that killed my brother; while to handle anything coated with rust was to risk having it enter my blood. There came a time, of course, I was about eighteen, when I realized that my fear of oxidized metal was utter nonsense. And then I realized that I'd been lied to for no apparent reason, which led me to wonder if there weren't perhaps other instances in which I'd been deliberately and without apparent good cause deluded.

When I finally had the nerve to ask Mu about the events surrounding Tai's death, Ba had been already dead for years. That fact and the genuine bafflement in my face and voice must have been what impelled her to answer a question concerning a topic she was unyield-

ingly silent about most of her life. She sighed and
threaded the needle in her hand. She started to say
something a few times, but stopped. She told me to take
my shirt off. Handing her my shirt, I showed where the
pocket had come off. Sensing I'd caught her in an unguarded moment and that she was on the verge of giving
me an answer, I pressed her again as to why we were forbidden to attend Tai's funeral. In the middle of mending
the shirt, she began to speak very slowly and quietly. *We,*
she began, *your father and I,* then she paused. *Your father
and I were very young,* she continued. *We were afraid of a
lot of things.* She never looked at me even once. She was
behaving as if she'd been caught at something, and her
voice was so naked in its shame and frustration that I felt
embarrassed to have asked the question. She continued,
*A lot of things scared us. We were scared all the time back
then.* I wanted her to stop. I felt the unkindness of my
original intention. She went on. *We were trying to protect
the rest of you. There was plenty of talk about the evil that
Tai's death might bring.* I was shocked, since Mu had ex-
pressed her total disregard for superstition. When I mentioned this, she grew impatient, admitting, *I was afraid.
And I really thought I would go insane from grief over Tai.* I
felt I'd gone too far with my mother. Yet I realized that
this was exactly what I had wanted from her. More than
the answer to why a long-past event turned out the way
it did, I wanted some sort of admission of guilt from Mu,
some expiation by pain. Now that Mu was giving it to
me, though, I could hardly receive it. I wanted her to
stop. But she would finish. *You can't know how bitter his*

death was to me. Then Mu handed me my shirt and, still not looking at me, whispered in a voice that would have sounded like a warning if she weren't talking about something in the past, *It was all bitter.*

The suspicion that much of what I'd lived by, much of what I'd lived believing, might have been the fabrications of adults who didn't recognize me enough to tell me the truth, had the same effect on me as the stories of Lammi and her sister Seeti. For while I suddenly began to feel hollow and insubstantial without the gravity of truth, I also began to feel more grounded, as though behind everything I'd called my life, including an episode in which my brother mysteriously, almost magically, dies of rust, lay Life, drastic and real, in which a boy dies of meningitis and his mother, young, separated from her husband and terrified by circumstances beyond her control, and exhausted by the demands of those circumstances, spontaneously concocts a lie. Having found life at that moment unmanageable, she created a manageable little story.

Though I know now he died of meningitis, to this day, I wonder if Tai was in much pain, and if it felt anything like the slow and steady eating away of iron.

Where is my father in all of this? His life remains, in greater part, hidden from me, and unspoken, since not speaking is a family trait, silence my inheritance, and since every time anyone ever talks, not just skeletons come jumping out of mouths, but doors and wardrobes and cars and trains and provinces and men and women and sex and madness and sex moneyed and money

sexed and money blooded and blood sexed and bodies
sexed and bodies moneyed, bodies coupled, bodies
cleaved, bodies sick, bodies abandoned like houses, and
houses, and cities and always one boy walking among
the bodies, one boy, my father, walking through the
houses, in the cities, sometimes beside his father, sometimes beside his mother who, whenever they pass young
couples on the streets, says to the boy without looking
down at him, *They are making a smelly doing, the smelly
woman and her stinking man*, his mother who sent him to
accompany his father in order to discourage his sexing
about, to discourage, not by words, his messy spattering
of seed, but by shame in the form of his son, but the
man, instead, is positively thrilled by the thought of his
thirteen-year-old boy waiting on the other side of a door
for him to finish his smelly business inside the woman
inside the room, yes, so thrilled is the man that years
later, at the age of eighty-two, fearing he has waned in
potency, he pays a boy to sit beside the bed of the young
woman he mounts and mounts without success, a boy
like his own, whom he made sit on "the tower" when he
misbehaved, perched for hours on a stool set atop a chair
set atop a desk set atop the dining table, teetering there,
eyes closed.

When I was six years old, two days after I arrived in
the United States with my family, my father's father
came in his car and took me, my sister, fourteen, and my
brothers, eight and three, to go live with him for two
weeks in a rundown apartment. We'd heard that our
grandfather was a rich man, so naturally we expected

the winged seed

something better as we rode in the roomy backseat of his Packard. But we also knew he was miserly, so we weren't surprised when we climbed a narrow stairs and entered that dive. We also knew enough to be afraid of him, since we'd gathered from whisperings and coded conversations between my parents that he was a pedophile, had spoiled plenty of young girls and boys in his time. He was also an embezzler and a swindler, had made a fortune trading in antiques, and was barely twenty when he had begun to plot his mother's murder in order to inherit the match factory her husband had left her when he died. A four-room business employing a dozen men, the match factory was the old woman's sole source of livelihood before she signed it over to her son in fear for her life. Why my parents let us go to live with him had something to do with my father's unshakable and ridiculous sense of filial piety, which Chinese of a feudal era hold above all other virtues. In the daytime, while our grandfather went to work, we stayed in the apartment. Not knowing English, and unfamiliar with the surroundings, we dared not venture out. Besides, he kept all of our shoes in a bathtub filled with water, which none of us were allowed to touch. He left a baked chicken in the refrigerator on which we gnawed a little each day, making it last. My sister, little soldier that she was, kept our spirits up by telling us stories, singing to us, and devising games to play. In the evenings, Yeh Yeh, my grandfather, came home with a woman he told us to call Auntie, though we knew she wasn't our aunt. Both of them walked around naked at all times, and encouraged us to do the same, but we said no. Yeh Yeh had a habit of coughing up large globs of phlegm and spitting them on the floor, which he told us to clean up, which we did. I swore when I grew up I would kill him with my bare hands. For years after that and well into adulthood, I dreamed I was beating him with a shoe heel. I would wake up screaming, exhausted.

Each night, before we went to bed, we were made to kneel before our dead grandmother's photograph and pray to it. There was a rumor that he had drowned his wife in an ice bath, so it felt strange to us to be praying to her, showing her this greatest respect at his behest when we believed he had perhaps killed her. Sometimes he broke into tears and kissed the photograph repeatedly. Perhaps it was then that I first began to despise my grandfather, wishing for the day I was big enough to confront him and knock him down. And when Yeh Yeh commanded that Fei sleep with him one night when Auntie wasn't there, I swore in my heart of hearts I'd chop the old man up and feed him to the birds, and never go home. But I didn't. There were no knives in the kitchen. There was nothing, no food, pots, pans. We drank from the tap with our hands.

When my father was a boy in China, that country was already old. When I say old I mean everything was there longer than anyone could recall, and all my father was born to was already worn out and passed to him, including his name, my blood. Especially his blood. Blood was the oldest thing and coursed inside him, making him already aged as a boy. He felt clogged with it and dammed with the talking about it. It was the blood telling its story. No blood, no story. There was a boy. And there was an old servant woman. And her telling began with blood. It always began with blood, the telling. The boy writes a word by drawing a symbol, a spear enclosed in a heart, piercing the heart from inside. And the servant woman nods and says the word, which means, in that singing tongue, *country*. It is my father's name. And there is a country, and, did I say this already, it is a very old country, against which a billion souls are in relief, a country which historical men have tried to affect or to own, without much avail on eternity. And Asay, the servant, is old, though not as old as that country, in which she stood each day of her tens of thousands of days, that country which encloses her snugly now underground. Old Asay, my grandfather's old servant, old gray head full of stories, enclosed now in this telling as earth encloses her bones and bone's stories. Asay, you were an old soul saying old things to my father about an old family of a country bound by blood, that flowed from the infinity of what's past into the headlong infinity of what's coming, the future here and here and here. Asay, your history of indentured service began before my father was born, when as a girl of sixteen, you were suddenly and simultaneously widow and sole survivor of your two-year-old boy's death. Either loss might have been enough to decide a woman's future anywhere in any time, but both losses at once in that country, and to such a young girl, determined absolutely and irrevocably your fate. There would be no appeals; you would enter the narrow destiny of your life as a servant in one of the Big Houses where you would become what is known in that country a "human to be used," and you would get used, and used up. You would get used efficiently and without passion or dreams or purpose on your part or on the part of those who used you. For that was the way with the Big Houses. That was the way in the Old Country. Yet there was affection between you and your first master's daughter; and when the daughter married a man from another clan, she took you with her into her husband's family. So that was how you learned the stories of both the Shaw *and* the Lee families, from talking that went on in kitchens and gardens, behind screens and doors, as well as the stories that were public knowledge, about these two families now brought together in the union of my grandmother and grandfather. Both families were merchants in the fishing industry, a lucrative and competitive business run mostly by large families of coarse stock. Fishermen and sailors, they eventually became gangsters and lords of the harbors, historical men whose creativity, ambition, and violence had finally little effect, or none at all in the world, all of them gone. The Houses gone, clans gone, titles gone, men gone, lords gone, the blood thinning, the telling broken.

Gone, the winter morning in the middle of the first half of the previous century, when two large groups of men met on a beachhead of a seaport town in the northwest of China. Gone, the men wrapped in cotton-padded, silk-lined coats and pants. Booted and bundled in animal skins and leather, they gathered without their

the

winged

seed

weapons to build a fire on the beach and boil a cauldron of oil. They fed the huge fire for hours before someone tossed in a handful of rice, which blackened instantly. Then everyone formed a great circle about the blowing and tearing flames, the logs burning loud and fast, fanned by sharp salt winds, while a neutral official stepped out of the crowd and yelled his statement over the crashing of fire and ocean and wind (gone the man's words): that the families Shaw and Kao, both gone now as I tell this, have met to end the war and determine once and for all which family would own the fishing rights to the waters they stood beside. Each family would choose one champion to decide the outcome, one man who was willing to put his arms past the elbows into the boiling oil, and then walk home unaided. Whichever man could do so won for his family all the waters, and anyone who fished those waters would pay a tax. Gone, the champions, who amounted to sacrificial victims. Two men stepped forward and faced each other on opposite sides of the steaming vat, their faces gnawed by days of fasting and ablutions, drinking and eating only specially prescribed herbs that dulled them to pain but sharpened their resolve to an inhuman determination. So they stood, fierce, self-murderous, dead already to everything except the accomplishment of this act which was necessarily a final act, ultimate.

Both men died, one before the other, the latter, my uncle, leaving behind for his family the rights to the sea, both men victims and perpetrators of the idea that the world exists by conflict and it was their duty to keep the balance between the clash of forces by prayer, vigil, and, most horrifyingly, sacrifice.

So the boy and the servant woman end at the end of the stories, and end with blood. The boy was the inheritor of the stories and Asay had inherited the telling of those stories. The blood, the blood is old, and a mystery. After each story, Asay would say to my father, *It's that blood, it's your blood.* And he would feel ancient, guessing at what she could mean.

It was just such stories my father contemplated as he listened outside a door to moaning, not female and heated, but cried out from another human wilderness, idiot babbling and screaming and chains rattling and the boy is forced to resee in his brain what he beholds with his eyes when at feeding time the great door, studded and lashed with metal bands, yawns open at the hands of Asay to a four-poster bed and its chained inmate, his gray hair shoulder-length, his face wispily bearded, his body sore-erupted and fetid, his brain daily nibbled by the worm which got inside him by way of a woman, the worm which, having made its slow, steady climb up the spine's intricate stair of nerves, began to excavate the tender brain, hollowing chambers, moving by the impulse of its insatiable, little-toothed appetite, to make of the gray matter a labyrinth of unparalleled and inimitable design, the way the devoured man's nephew, the little boy's father, ate his way through women, many and faceless, and in chambers of many hallways, his phallus shrugging and shivering its way inside, so lonely it was.

the
winged
seed

Here, I lie untouched, vague to myself. I am a sliver secreted in flesh. A thorn riding in *R*'s thigh. I am here, in a gouged place, and the light carmine. Mere hearsay is blue, that true and intensest glistening of morning, mere hearsay the great, occasional pulse I sometimes approximate my whereabouts by. Narrow is how I lie without you, Donna, shaved to an excellent shard to fit this slit of dark meantime. Here, no past, no future, all occurrence *not yet*, or else *already*, and the not yet trickles backward into the already. And it all runs away. The time and space we span is what we'll eventually lose. Yet, lessening increases our gravity, Love. And all we ever really possess is a rude thirst and hunger. And though this room encloses us, and is furthermore enclosed by the city, which is gathered in the dark, which overcomes us entirely, my desire for you exceeds even this city. In that fact do I take comfort. And in my chief end: to drive deeper toward any rumored heart.

Here, there is no sleep. I remember Sabbath mornings and how, before the tolling of the call to worship, at which moment I would emerge in my robe from a door behind the pulpit and light the candles set the width of the altar, my father's bells chimed a pretty tune, a melody full of distances and the invisible, his bells so full of space and echoes. The time the tune lasted was always just enough time for me to walk up the stairs from Sunday school, put on my robe, light my wick, and wait one second in the archway of the little door behind the pulpit.

But one morning I found a girl waiting for me on the

stairs as I walked up. She stood blocking my way, and though I couldn't see her face in that lightless flight, I knew who she had to be, and imagined her face, and could tell by something in her voice that she was smiling.

Quick, she said, *kiss me here*, and pointed with a dark finger to her mouth.

On these stairs? I asked, terrified.

On these dark stairs, she answered, standing straight up and still, so that I, three steps lower, would have to step up and then stretch a little to reach her face with my face, put my mouth over her mouth.

In the length of that kiss, the bells had ended their prelude, were already into the seventh toll, and all of the old fathers and old mothers, the good and faithful, were staring horrified at the unlit altar, the centuries-old dark of a cave in which the table stood, the chalice, the old book, the cross.

That afternoon, Ba whipped me with his belt until both of our foreheads broke out in salt.

In him was my beginning. From him I rose. Naturally, his body interested me continually. I preserved the hairs I found on his pillow every morning. I washed his feet in a basin of water and trimmed the thick nails of his two big toes with little black Chinese scissors. Versed in its needs and weight, I carried it on my back to the bathroom and back when he was bedridden. I memorized his medicines and their proper dosages. I helped him organize drawerfuls of tablets and capsules, dividing them into daily requirements, the tiny blue lasix, the little bitter cortisone, his breath become chemical exhalations, acrid. The roses by his bed, thriving on aspirin, never opened.

But what do such stories have to do with me now? My love, this is a story about dying. A story I tell myself when, in a darkened room whose one window looks out to a brick wall, I can't sleep. This is not, however, a story about death. But dying. Dying is all, the earth filling with us, who fill the sky with news of it. But only birds can reveal to us dying. By flying. And so our eyes open to transparencies, hollow bones. The flight is nothing, the pattern. Aren't the turns and dives overhead shed as well as fled, husk, merely what what's left behind by the dying? Isn't dying what we're doing? For dying occurs exactly at the bird. Did I say bird?

I meant word. This is a story about a word, one word. Dying occurs exactly at the word. Neither before nor after. Neither in the anticipation of its saying, nor in the silence afterward. To read such dying as it occurs in the field of the air, to divine meaning, is to stay with the body of the bird at every moment of its newness, every instant of the turn, the glance, the bird its gestures. The word is itself, and gathers unto itself pure turn, sheer glance, true bird opening in violence at the very brink of the dying bird, who is nothing if not the assembly of glance, thrust, and turn. The way the bird fills the dying out, the way it is equal to the dying at every place: there, there, there. It can not disappoint the flying, for it dies it. And such dying is saying. Such saying must be possible, so saying might achieve a *here* and *now*, so saying *is*. There is no horizon in this saying, only the dying without remainder. There is no horizontal groping from *here* to *there*, no allegorical grasping after a *that* from *this*. And the word as it is saying is the very ground, not the same as the word as it was said. Only the word saying is both present and actual. When the bird is dying, the bird is not dead. The word dead is altogether another thing than the bird dying. And when the bird stands at rest, no flying is disclosed, though the sky remains filled with news of our passing. When the bird is dying, there is flying. But there is rest in flying, too. There is the rest of the body residing in its dying. There is the rest of the word standing in its saying. This is not the same rest as the word standing unsaid, a cessation from saying. This is a resting within the saying. Not the rest of your body next to me, restless in its turning and dreaming and sweating and grinding of teeth. This is a story I tell myself when I'm restless. This is a story about rest. The rest in saying, my love.

But whose hand is it now I see holding a pencil and moving over a piece of paper, delineating a body? I see a girl holding a train ticket. It is Fei. She is standing under the windowed arch of Union Station, where the stairs descend from four compass points to converge on the marble floor, so everyone may come together a moment before they scatter on trains bound in all directions of the earth. And all of those languages spoken by all of those mouths rise toward the ceiling, where they convene and are understood in a way they are not on the ground. On the dull marble floor of the train station, it is my mother standing with one boy on her hip, two more alongside, and her daughter of fourteen, all of us waiting for my father, who has gone to ask how long until the next train. Our hair is full of shadows, our eyes. A little pool of shadow for each mouth. When my father comes back, his coat pockets are full of oranges. It's his hand! It's my father's hand moving over a page of his drawing book, making me disappear in order that I might finally arrive at what I am, fruit scoured to pit. I remember when, from upstairs, my father called, and I went. I went fearful and a little nauseated. For I knew what he had in store, that old alchemist. He would make me disappear. By his voice and with his fierce heart, under the hard wooden gaze of his one blind eye and in the presence of his God, he would abolish me.

Disappearing is a cinch. I should know, I did it by dummying up. For the first three years of my life, I made not a sound. After that I was frequently plagued by long periods of dumbness, up until I was seven or eight. But Ba would have nothing of my muteness. He would have me whole, healed, my tongue unstuck, that stubborn, unresponsive muscle thick inside my head. He would free for me the useless, indolent worm behind my teeth. So he put his hands on me, his own defective flesh, and prayed a hard, frothy stream of hardly intelligible words.

But why should I have spoken? Why should I have loosened and rattled for him, entered the traffic of talk, of indirection, the approximate, the almost? Why, when my silence was so present, so irreducible and true? Why, when my silence, like rock that's rock clear through, was silence so final? I was immaculate. Language couldn't cling to my bald tongue.

So, in Hong Kong, once a week, I sat in a chair and let him put the palm of one of his big hands on the back of my head and the other over my mouth, while Mu, Fei, and Go sat in their assigned chairs as witnesses, for where two or three are gathered, there a miracle might occur. Then Ba shut his eyes tight, so tight his brow looked cut with lines, bowed his head, and, grumbling and hissing, intoned his prayer that a voice come into me, or out of me. To be touched thus, to have my entire mouth seized in his hand, was almost too much. I almost said a word. But I did not, my tongue paralyzed, my voice so gone. Even Ba could not draw a voice out of me. For where talk was disappointing, my silence would never disappoint me. I could build a table on it, and chairs, a house, throw a party, people would bring their talk, waves of it, volumes of bright ephemera, all of it hovering on the surface of what was deepest. Talk was hovering, skirting, glancing. Talk was mere. And I wouldn't. And because I didn't, everyone hid nothing from me. Not that they trusted me; they didn't. Not that they should have, since I was building a case against most of them. But because I didn't, everyone was free to say anything at all in front of me. And there were those who were somehow convinced that my stricken mouth was a sign of my stupidity. Believing that my being dumb meant my being dumb, they grew used not only to saying but to doing whatever came to mind while I was there.

As if, because I could not relay what I saw or heard, all I saw or heard was safe with me, or dead in me: a servant's small theft in the kitchen, a cabby's hand on the cook's new breasts. Because I could not speak, I could not judge, I was an end, stopped. So they hoped. And it's true, I was opaque. Nothing passed through me. I only absorbed, contained, without emanation or ejaculation. So, I grew in the core of my silent self, denser and denser with sound. For there was sound all around and I could hear it. There, on my wall, the gecko spoke, and I heard my fine pet. There, over me, my mother was kissing me, and I could hear her. There, in the garden, the leaves moved and I could hear them. Over the garden wall, the bicycle bells rang, and I heard them. The rains came hard and I heard them driving down on each roof and leaf. There, always over *there*, was sound, and I could hear it. But *here*, where I lived with me, was silence. I could hear the servants gossiping over there. I could hear the lice popping between fingernails when they cleaned them from one another's scalps. I could hear them dragging combs dipped in coconut oil through one another's straight black hair. But it was all over there. *Here* was I, unto myself. And my silence was larger than myself. Larger even than Mu and Ba, my silence could contain them, and everything else. I could hold everything without changing it into words, without violating it. Unlike Ba, who changed everything at will with his voice.

If he cleared his throat I would stop, wait, then proceed, pushing my truck across the floor of his study. He could revise the day with a word, and the only warning, if there was any at all, might be something as negligible as him clearing his throat.

Everything depended on Ba: if we went to bed hungry or full, beaten or spared. And Fei, Go, and I learned to read not only him, but the very air about him, a palpable element when he was present in it. We could detect the least change in the weather in the rooms of his house, and we didn't have to be in the same room with him. Our life was his rage. We studied it, watched it, detected its slightest adumbrations and slimmest quakings. Like a scaly-taloned, hard-beaked bird, his wrath came sudden, heralded briefly only by a palest shadow, an almost unnoticeable darkening of the day, before the shattering entrance. And we withstood it to the best of our separate capacities.

But it was I, Mu told me once, who broke my father's rage. *Your father was a blade*, Mu said, *and he broke against you upon continual sharpening, you are so hard and obdurate.*

So he broke against me! So he was a blade, my bright-edged Ba! So I kept him sharp! But it wasn't hardness on my part, I should have told Mu. It was capacity and willingness. A willingness not to flee him. I would not flee the cloud over his forehead. I would not fear his fierce blind eye, nor his roving, seeing pupil. And in his last years, when he grew weak, when he was like some fledgling, I resented his decline. *Raise up!* I wanted to yell. *I'm still here! Get on with the forging and making of father and son!* For Mu must have been right. Didn't I participate in my father's making? Didn't his flesh eat mine in order to get on with its life? And when he was eating me, wasn't I quiet? Though he yelled, *Brave boy won't cry? Good! I'll beat you until you cry out!* But I did not cry out. Because it was my strength he admired and loved, and I would be what he admired, I would be his beloved. And because I was determined that *he* must cry out. After all, wasn't it his own voice he desired to hear? Wasn't it his own cry he was trying to pare me down to? And I knew that the only way he would expel his own cry was if I held out, if I let him glut himself on me until he could not stand it and then yelled *Enough!* So I vowed in silence, *You must beat me, Ba, until you cry out! For there is, I know, one cry inside you. And now I will help you utter it.*

But Ba did not utter it. Instead, Ba sweat. He hit me until his forearms sweat. Then he threw his belt at the wall and walked away.

But in his last years, when I bathed him, and washed the head I was never allowed to stand above, and shaved the face I was never allowed to touch even with my lips, I thought about the islands, how when he strode down the aisle of his church, the believers reached out their hands to touch him. I thought about how he ascended the altar and sent up his spirit in a torrent of crashing nonsense. And at the baptismal well, the believers crowded the edges in their white robes, some falling in at him, who stood, waist-deep in water, his own white robe billowing like a flower all around him, his arms outstretched to receive them, who came and came. They saw how he nearly drowned their brothers and sisters, and they came toward the water. They watched how he wrestled the hesitant, and they proceeded to the well. They worshiped and feared him. They loved him. How could I do less? How could I ever flee all of that excellent power? So I fellowed Ba's wrath, though I lived in horror of the tuition, in fear of his countenance, that countenance which beseeched the Holy Spirit to free my tongue.

But what had I to say, anyway? Didn't everyone say it all, over and over again? The declarations, the orders, the requests, the questions, the whispers; all of it a distraction from that true speech occurring prior to talk, all of it meant to assault what was absolute, what was eternal and back of words. So much in terror of the perfect, they would adorn it with words, circumvent it with inaccuracies. But if I refused to speak, who could convince me otherwise? Not even Ba, or Ba's God, could make me surrender my ground, my silence.

But years later, in his room, where he sat in one corner, and I sat at his too-large desk, in a too-big chair, typing out the sermons he'd composed on the tongue, typing draft after draft, I was disappearing. Even as my body ached in its growth, I was already becoming invisible, for I was nowhere to be found. Nowhere except in those drawings he made of me; and even now I am nowhere in my own memories of those days, so many of them they all run together into one endless day inside my father's room, where either his voice is speaking or his hand is moving, making a picture, picture after picture.

Sometimes, as I sat for him to draw, my thoughts strayed and I followed them out of my body, until I was called back by his voice saying, *Close your mouth* or *You moved your head*, while his hand continued to move, his eyes holding me still. He saw all of me, looking directly at me but at no particular part of me.

Once, he drew for nearly an hour with a deepening frown on his face, and then leaped at me so suddenly I sat rigid in alarm. He bent down and, with his front teeth, bit off a loose thread hanging from the sheet draped across my lap. When he got back to work his frown was gone. That was how I learned patience. Some days he worked in such unbroken fury he had to lie down on the couch afterward.

I remember how on certain Sunday evenings he would show us his best-loved possessions, unrolling across our dining-room table the hundred-year-old scrolls he'd carried over the sea from China. He showed them to us in the order he remembered having collected them, and the first one, unscrolled, revealed first the black claws, and then the long legs, and at last the whole height of a standing crane, long-beaked, with coarse head and neck feathers, and one fierce eye. The second scroll was mostly white except for the blight-struck pine, and one bird perched at the tip: a shrike, surviving, last carrier of seed and stones in his little gizzard. The scrolls in my father's house, stored in room after room, or hung in the halls, were so many any breeze could send their silk dancing and their bones all knocking against the walls. He spent every day in August, his vacation time, painting from

morning to evening, filling sheet after sheet of rice paper
with washes of ink. I watched him lean over the table
and his hand flee, or seem to flee, the ink running past
the brush and into the very bird. It was birds he painted,
one after another. *To make you see flying in a standing
body*, he said, his arm moving up and down to be flying,
pushing backward to be drawing nigh, backing up into
the future in order to be coming into what's passed. One
human hand, a bird, resigned to let time resolve it in paper and ink. It takes one bird to write the central action
of the air, lending its wings to gravity, in order to be aloft.

But *Wait*, says the seed in my hand, *It is not time to fly.
Tell me a story.*

What story do you need to hear? The news on the radio is the flight out from Pharaoh and Sukarno continues, and our cousins are being smuggled with the other
perishable cargo, rope, rain, and sacks of rice; and as
long as the harbors are dark, herds flee out from Asia,
wearing her necklace of skulls, doomed Europe and her
ovens full, Mother Russia scouring the back steps with
wire and broom, the fly-bitten eyelids of Africa; while
David waits for Jonathan in a cave, Joseph interprets the
foreigner's dreams, my father is missing and no one
knows where he is. My brother has died and is to be
buried at two. My father has been moved to a hospital
for the insane. Not because he was mad, my mother re-
minds me, but because he discovered that having his status changed from political prisoner to hospital patient
gained him visitation rights. My sister remembers that
our mother visited him almost every day and sometimes

we accompanied her, to sit at a round metal table in a little courtyard surrounded by a covered walk. To get there we were led down a hall of cell doors. Each door had a tiny barred window and as we walked we could hear echoing the entire length of the hall the moans and screams and babbling coming from the locked cubicles. In the yard we were left alone to wait for my father, who came escorted by one hospital employee. The only soldiers we saw were at the hospital entrance. There, in the sunlight, every day for almost a year, my parents hatched schemes to leave the island. Since the more docile patients of the hospital were permitted to roam the yard, we were never alone, but always sat in the midst of half a dozen crazy people. Some of them walked in circles, some of them mumbled to themselves, some of them giggled uncontrollably. All of them were ashen, disheveled men in rags. Sometimes they begged for food or tried to talk to us. They weren't the violent patients, and so weren't considered dangerous, but they frightened us anyhow, one of them talking to us with his eyes rolled back in his head, his eyelids fluttering with only the whites exposed, another acting perfectly normal except he kept interrupting his sentences with spitting and high-pitched squealing fits. Sometimes a group of orderlies walked by and nodded to us politely, each carrying a long stick made out of rattan. They were on their way to administer the regular morning beatings. Soon we would hear the howls coming from deep inside the hospital. Beating was considered a cure for certain disorders. The feeling among the staff was that most of the patients only needed encouragement to overcome their condition. Encouragement came in the form of thrashing with rattan sticks, or lecturing, which consisted of a staff member standing over a seated patient and screaming at him for half an hour about what a disgrace he was, while the patient sat either weeping and promising to reform his ways or nodding absently with his jaw hanging slack. None of these practices were considered shameful, so they were conducted openly, even in plain view of the other patients, to serve as examples. When a group of journalists and photographers from Europe and the United States visited, however, a volleyball net was set up in the yard, and beer and peanuts were served to the inmates. Since some of the patients were regularly rousted in the middle of the night and whipped, the screaming, my father told us, could be heard all night long.

Much is unclear to me concerning that time, 1959. I know, however, that my father started preaching in the hospital. In the same yard we visited him in, he sat and talked about the Kingdom of God, at first only to the crazies, but later, even hospital staff came to hear him. After some time, even the guards at the hospital entrance referred to him with affection, even with respect, as Rabbi. He preached once a week in the crowded yard, reciting huge passages he'd memorized of the King James Bible. From the numbers of those who were there like my father as political prisoners, he made a few friends. It was a group of these friends who, after their release, wrote my father a farewell letter the day before they left the island. My father read that letter to me years later, weeping in his house in Pennsylvania. In it, they called him Beloved Rabbi. All of them and their families were killed when the boat they were on was stopped a few miles out of port, everyone on it was searched, and the soldiers opened fire.

My father attributed his survival and our escape to miracles by a divine hand. So naturally, for a time, I imagined a scene in which the guards fall asleep and his cell door swings open mysteriously. What actually happened, in fact, seems no less providential when viewed in the context of what had become, for many Chinese like my parents, a hopeless predicament. Escape was impossible, the purge had begun, weapons were being handed out to farmers as well as thugs, and all over the island, agents of the president were preaching the evils of Chinese and other foreigners. My mother, recalling that time, says there was not a single possible step to be taken in any direction. What was obviously about to happen, chaos and killing, had already begun. The War Administration was bent on prosecuting all suspects. Their promise was to miss no one. There were rumors of executions, though no one we knew had yet been killed. It wasn't until many years later that we heard who lived and died. But house-to-house roundups had already begun, and homes were even being plundered by the soldiers. Our own home had been visited numerous times by soldiers working for themselves. They asked for furniture and money. My mother surrendered some tables and chairs once, and a few dollars on a number of occasions. Most of the time, we kept the front gate locked and the house dark. In the meantime, my mother's efforts to get our father's release were useless. At one point, she was told by administration officials that all she needed to do was collect a certain number of signatures attesting to her husband's innocence and good character. But everyone she went to, mostly colleagues from the university, was either locked up or too intimidated to sign the forms.

One day, my father told my mother she should get everything in order so that we could leave the island. Rumor said we would soon be shipped to Macau, where we would be given quarters and remain under arrest, prisoners of Sukarno, enemies of Indonesia. Since we would only be allowed to bring a few things, our preparations would include liquidating as many assets as possible without suspicion and finding a way to transport relatively large sums of cash and gold without being found out. That meeting with my father was her last with him in the little yard. When she came back the next day, she was told she could no longer see him. A month went by, during which my mother could not get news from anyone, and one day a man from the War Administration came to our house and informed us my father had died. He told us we would have to move out of our house as soon as possible. After he left, my mother told us not to believe him. She didn't believe our father dead, and she would not let that man take our house. She continued preparations just as she and my father had planned. She had a special leg brace designed to replace my sister's old brace. The new one had a hollow sole built into the footpiece where pieces of gold were wedged. Wads of bills replaced the stuffing in my sister's doll, and more money was sewn into the collars of our coats. Rumors began to circulate that my father in fact was dead and that soon the soldiers would come to take our house. Nights, I dreamed a man who looked nothing like my father, but answering to his name, stood at the back door knocking.

I slept as a child with my brothers and sister and our mother, in a walled and perfect place, perfect because square. Out of one of the walls two doorways were cut, like strange emblems standing as far apart from each other as possible; on fearful nights the doors could seem like long hands held up in surrender or worship, the face of the wall illegible between them. Directly opposite that wall was the one window, paneless, over the sill of which a gecko entered by moonlight to climb to a corner near the ceiling and cling to its shadow until dawn. Under the window, spanning the width of the wall and claiming over half the room, was the bed, a teak platform supporting large futons on which was spread a mat of cool rattan on which to sleep through hot nights at the equator. By the bed was a wooden nightstand, beautifully carved by an unknown and imperfect hand, on which stood a drinking glass and a pitcher of water with a handkerchief covering its mouth.

The window looked out onto an alley of stamped earth and the back gates of three homes that belonged to the Engs, a Chinese couple who owned the all-night shopping bazaar called Happy World, the Lins, another Chinese couple, and Aba, a Javanese woman whose last name we never knew.

Framed by her gate, Aba's face appeared each night behind a curl of smoke and the glowing eye of a cigarette, and out of her plush mouth came the little thread of sound *Selamat malan*, over and over again, repeated to the passersby. All night long, brown-toothed Aba presided at the edge of the alley, her flabby, ample flesh bearing down on the little stool on which she squatted while she smoked, or chewed and spat tobacco like a corpulent grasshopper, always greeting the passersby with *A peaceful night to you*, in a tongue that rang of pilgrimages, uncharted deserts, veiled faces beyond lion-colored walls.

Aba, we were told, was a member of one of the oldest families in our village, with a long line of ancestors whose affairs were graced by divine intervention. Rumor had it that Aba had in her employment a very powerful spirit who made sure she prospered. That was how she was able to live in such a fine house without ever having to work. There was a man named Hardo something or other, Aba's grandfather's grandfather, who practiced Islam in the late sixteenth century and recited a version of a prayer which derived from Portuguese spice traders for whom Hardo as a young man sailed as cabin boy. One morning, Aba told us, the boy escaped violence on the docks, outbursts more and more frequent, eventuating in the ousting of the Portuguese from Indonesia altogether. Hardo's European master was found dead in his cabin. Inches in him, to cleave his sternum, was a rhinoceros horn, coincident with Java's liberation, and the dawn of a purer configuration of Islam on that island of Hardo's heart. He studied prayer and the arts of magic and healing. He passed down the prayers to subsequent family members, and by the time Aba had learned a portion of the prayer from her father, Hardo's grandson, who was neither devout nor prayerful, the meaning of the words was long forgotten.

But *Selamat malan*, Aba intoned to a continuous stream of walkers passing beneath our window, strolling, or on their way home from the all-night shadow plays. All through the night we heard Aba, and all seemed safe, we felt attended to by that outside voice and what it said to no one in particular, everyone who passed, anyone who heard.

It's exhausting, mistress, she'd once exclaimed to my Mu, *I bless them all who pass by and do not miss one all night*, as though she were some sort of sentinel whose job it was to sow nocturnal benedictions.

On either side of her, the homes of the Lins and the Engs had been ransacked by soldiers. Both old Lin and old Eng had been arrested. Mrs. Lin lived alone and Mrs. Eng had recently been committed to an insane asylum after she locked all of the servants inside the house and tried to set fire to the place. She frequently went crazy, but before her husband was taken, he protected her and cared for her. One day she was found running naked through the streets, ranting that a demon had seduced her in the outhouse. Mr. Eng, with the help of

several other men, caught her, bound her, and took her
home, where a specialist was summoned, an old man
Aba had recommended, who had cured many, and who,
Aba claimed, was a distant uncle. He diagnosed Mrs.
Eng's case as demon possession, and he interrogated the
demon.

Where are you from?

From the ruins, the unwanted visitor of Mrs. Eng's
body replied.

Will you please go back to where you came from?

If you feed me.

So Aba's famous uncle tickled Mrs. Eng's nose with a
corner of an ancient sarong he'd pulled from his bag, and
when she was about to sneeze he blew into her open
mouth a handful of incense, at which the woman
gagged, coughed, took a sip of brandy held at the ready
by her husband, and fell asleep. She woke in a few minutes refreshed and without any knowledge of the event.

But with her husband gone, she was a danger to herself and everyone around her. So she was taken away and
locked up. Mu took the news to her husband, who was
being kept in the same prison as Ba. It was months after
the fact before Mu was able to get a message to Mr. Eng.
Weeping, he asked about Mu and her children, then
thanked her for bringing him news of his wife. Their
house stood empty of them and most of their furniture.

On the other side of Aba, Mrs. Lin played her
phonograph at full blast every afternoon. She was a
strict Buddhist and vegetarian whose favorite pastime
was concocting various recipes of wheat gluten that

were meant to look and taste like meat. She loved to invite Fei, Go, and I to her house to taste the results. After appetizers of French butter and fruit preserves spread on English biscuits, we sampled the doughy slices of starch cut from gluten sculptures that looked like a duck or a fish or a pig. The eyes of the animals were made of prunes and raisins. It was like eating her collection of toy animals, and they all tasted like unleavened bread boiled in soy sauce. But we accepted her invitations, for we loved to watch her make the gluten, which she did while we ate. The entire kitchen was covered in flour, and huge kettles of flour and water were waiting for her hands to season and knead. And we loved to listen to her sing along with the songs she played on the phonograph. We begged her to sing for us, at which requests she at first demurred and then answered wholeheartedly by launching with both of her lungs into awful renditions of "Once I Had a Secret Love," or "The River of No Return," while sloshing around elbow-deep in six separate kettles of water and flour, adding more water, punching and pulling the mountains of sticky dough in order to get the right consistency, while Fei served us more crackers spread with a quarter inch of the delicious French butter and good dollops of preserves. And though all three of us laughed out loud, it never seemed to bother Mrs. Lin or convince her that she sounded anything but exactly like Doris Day or Marilyn Monroe.

I remember lying awake at night, trying to remember what Ba looked like, and finding a blank space where his

face should have been. What most disturbed me was
that it wasn't perfectly blank, but seemed to suggest fea-
tures. There I lay trying to focus on what might have
been a mouth, or eyes, or a nose, turning the image this
way and that in my mind, holding it closer and farther,
hoping to catch just one clear glimpse of that face that
was supposed to belong to my father. At times the face
became a leaf, and I got lost studying the intricate arter-
ies and veins. Sometimes it became the face of a stranger
I might have seen at the bazaar, having noticed a face
that looked vaguely like Ba's. Sometimes my mind was
blank, and as I tried to focus I realized I was looking at a
cloud, just a shadowy cloud where a face should have
been.

In the spell of Aba's blessing each night, *Selamat
malan,* I lay awake in the dark, searching my heart for a
face I recognized, while Mu sat propped against the wall
slowly fanning herself with the big banana leaf fan. *Selu-
mat malan,* as the room filled with our heavy breathing
as one by one we fell asleep. *Selamat malan,* and beyond
Aba's voice, from some other house, always came the
strains of someone singing a song. Nights in Jakarta were
filled with human sounds; not the racket of urban
dwellings, but the sounds of other lives proceeding, a
whole world of voices speaking outside the window,
singing in the distance, calling someone home, passing
over our sleep. And though I was mute my first few years
of life, could not utter any of those human noises, I
heard them fully, and as I listened to Aba, I began to
match her sounds to letters my mother taught us—the

two words she spoke, *s-e-l-a-m-a-t-m-a-l-a-n*. Twelve letters put together, seven to the first word, five to the second. Then I put the letters of the first word into alphabetical order: *a-e-l-m-s-t*. Then the letters of the second word: *a-a-l-m-n*. But something was wrong. Spelled out, the letters of the first word totaled seven. In alphabetical order, they totaled six on my fingers. Which letter was missing? I repeated the process and discovered I'd forgotten an *a*. Now I had it right: *a-a-e-l-m-s-t*. And as I listened to Aba repeat the words, I repeated silently to myself the letters in the order I'd put them, over and over, *aaelmst, aalmn*. After many nights, I discovered I could do this with great speed and accuracy to any random word or short phrase spoken in Javanese, spelling the words out as I counted their number on my fingers, and then rearranging the letters in alphabetical order. Sometimes I'd wonder what the words sounded like spoken the way I'd spelled them. I lay many nights wondering if in fact I hadn't discovered a great secret code embedded in the very alphabet and the words we spoke. But since I couldn't talk, I couldn't communicate this discovery to anyone. Neither could I actually hear what the words sounded like. I could only look at them in my mind. I challenged myself sometimes by laying the words of a phrase side by side and putting all the letters of the phrase into alphabetical order. Of the things I remember most about that time, this obsessive mental habit remains the most vivid to me. I remember how the letters would pile up in my mind, meaningless except for the order they reflected. It was a habit I con-

l
i
.
y
o
u
n
g

l
e
e

tinued for almost thirty years. Frequently, a series of letters remained with me long after I'd forgotten what
those letters, unscrambled, might have signified at one
time. So it was very possible that I might forget that the
series *aaegillm* was the alphabetical ordering of the letters which made up the word *Gamaliel*, in which case I
would for days recall *aaegillm*, repeating the series over
and over like some sort of talisman, or like the rungs of a
ladder or keys of a piano as my fingers moved in their
counting and my mind picked over again and again,
without significance, the letters.

One night I did what was expressly forbidden to me. I
spelled Ba's name. Since none of us were allowed to refer
to Mu or Ba in any manner other than as Mu or Ba, such
an act felt dangerous to me. Not even allowed to speak
of them using the third person pronoun or speak to
them using the second person pronoun, to say their
proper names felt criminal to me. But I reasoned that I
was not committing an offense because I was not actually speaking his name. I spelled his name in Javanese,
and then put the letters in alphabetical order: *aaeejlry*.
In lieu of his face, then, I concentrated on this his name,
and I shortened it, dropping the extra *a* and *e* to make:
aejlry. And then I spelled the letters themselves: *a-e-j-a-
y-e-l-a-r-w-i*, and memorized that sequence: *aejayelarwi*,
and then alphabetized it: *aaaeeijlrwy*. I felt sure it was an
auspicious accident that this version of Ba's name
should have a series of three vowels repeated in diminishing numbers, three *a*'s, two *e*'s, and one *i*, and noted
how the letters that followed the *i* were, in fact, at least

to my eye, gradual permutations of the letter *i*. I imagined the letter *i* growing a curly tail to become a *j*, then drawing the tail back into itself and stretching itself to touch the dot above it to become the column of *l*. I repeated my father's new name in my mind: *aaaeeijlrwy*. There were nights I spelled the letters out and repeated the process, endlessly, into infinity, Aba's blessing standing next to me as I proceeded to sleep.

Night. Mother wren, soldier heron, and pastor crow were all three waiting for citizen seed to wake, to rise from his dark bed walking, to speak. The seed lay in a dead swoon. Somewhere, snow fell past a clock, and the seed slept. Somewhere, a man grew a beard and died in his cell, and the seed slept. A woman waited for her lover a lifetime, then swept her kitchen of leaves blown in from seasons upon seasons of trees the man left unpruned, the shears hung to rust in a lower branch, and the seed slept. A city closed its gates. The seed slept. *What to do?* fretted mother wren. *Stand fast*, counseled the heron. The pastor, wise crow, spoke: *Only a hand can help us, and only a thief. For only a thief will know the way into a fortified seed. But where*, asked the soldier, *will we find such a hand?*

The wren looked here and there, in a hayloft, inside an old coat sleeve. The pastor ventured throughout the countryside. The heron guarded the sleeper. One night the crow found the hand lying under a thigh. The hand smelled of oranges and fish, and lay dreaming of oranges bobbing in the ocean, among the wreckage of crates, the fruit nudged now and then from below, nibbled by un-

l
i

•

y
o
u
n
g

l
e
e

seen mouths. The crow scratched a message on the windowsill, tapped on the pane, then fled. The hand, a blind thief, read the pecked sill with its fingers, then lit out after the bird.

After many years the bird and the hand arrived where the tattered wren, in a cap of snow, stood by the heron, who wore a shawl of snow across his powerful shoulders. *There*, said the crow to the thief, and the hand approached the tiny sleeper.

Children, I know you wonder how a hand may enter a place so narrow as a seed. The answer is the hand must die. So the hand lay down next to the seed, opened, and the three ravenous birds ripped up its flesh and gobbled up the blood, and put the bones in a sack.

Once inside the seed, the thief, who had been blind, could see. He moved toward the heart of the seed, but found his path blocked by a book. Leafing through the book, he noticed many pages missing. Yet, even with missing pages, the book was too large to move, too high to vault, and too wide to go around. So he sat down and began to read the book with the missing pages. Reading first the odd-numbered pages, and then the even, he read out loud, while all one hundred rooms of the house of the seed echoed with the sound of a hand reading.